Life & Times Series

Freightliner

Class 47 No.47008 works the Coatbridge-Felixstowe Freightliner at Levington on the Felixstowe branch, 15th April 1987.

Michael J. Collins

Class 47 No.47333 is seen at Ripple Lane FLT with 4O89, the 15.06 (SO) Freightliner for Southampton (Maritime), 10th September 1988.

Michael J. Collins

Life & Times Series

Freightliner

Michael J. Collins

Oxford Publishing Co.

A FOULIS-OPC Railway Book

British Library Cataloguing in Publication Data
Collins, Michael J. (Michael James) *1947 –*
    Freightliners
    1. Great Britain. Railway services: British Rail. Freight rolling stock
    I. Title   II. Series
    625.24094
    ISBN 0-86093-455-1

Library of Congress catalog card number
90-84487

Published by:
Haynes Publishing Group
Sparkford, Near Yeovil, Somerset. BA22 7JJ

Haynes Publications Inc.
861 Lawrence Drive, Newbury Park, California 91320, USA.

Printed by: J.H. Haynes & Co. Ltd
Typeset in 9/10pt Univers Medium Roman

Contents

Every weeknight two Freightliner trains head from Coatbridge to Felixstowe. Here, the second service which had left Scotland at 20.54 the previous evening passes the wayside station at Kennett, near Newmarket, in June 1987. Traction on this occasion was provided by Class 47 No.47307.

Michael J. Collins

Introduction and Acknowledgements

The Freightliner system is based on the carriage of high-capacity boxes or containers on specially-designed rail wagons capable of operation at speeds up to 75mph. Like service passenger trains the Freightliner trains run in fixed formations and to an agreed timetable, in an attempt to provide a fast and reliable service over long and medium distances at low cost. Today, most of the containers carried meet International Standards Organisation (ISO) specifications and aim to make possible the most efficient use of all transport modes whether by rail, road or sea.

November 1990 was the 25th anniversary of the introduction of the Freightliner concept. Railfreight Distribution is justifiably proud of this arm of its services as one of the pioneers of the world wide container concept and it is proud also of its achievements over the last quarter of a century.

This book aims to trace the development of Freightliner through the last twenty-five years, first as an independent subsidiary of the British Rail Board and later, as an important component in the Railfreight Distribution network. It also looks at a selection of the associated spin off containerisation by private enterprise where it is relevant to rail transport in Britain. During the last twenty-five years of development many changes have taken place within the industry but so succesful has the concept been that container movements in the United Kingdom (and, indeed, in the world) have been increasing rapidly as every year has passed by.

But most of all the Freightliner arm of Railfreight Distribution is considered to be unique. Freightliner customers do not think of the enterprise as a road haulier, nor as an arm of the railways. Freightliner has come to be regarded as simply "Freightliner". The word conjures up the intermodal transport sytem which it portrays. Freightliner has spread its influence far and wide and is highly respected in the fiercely competitive transport market. Fuel cost increases have heightened competitiveness, and this is specially true over long distances. The introduction of EEC regulations on lorry drivers' hours has enabled this arm of the railway network to outstrip the road hauliers on price on journeys over about 450 kilometres.

I must take this opportunity to thank the many individuals who have helped me with this book. In particular Mr David Green of Railfreight Distribution deserves special thanks because he has supported the project since its inception, organised the cab ride for me and sent me on trips to various Freightliner terminals. He also allowed me to browse through the photograph collection at Freightliner headquarters and suffered my fool questions without complaint all day. The many photographers who have opened up their valuable collections for my use need thanking as does Mr Roger Silsbury who kindly offered his expertise and wrote the chapters on the railway wagons and containers. My good friend and photographic companion, Mr John Day of Ipswich, was invaluable in reading the text and his eagle eye and helpful advice was much appreciated. My wife, Margaret, also needs a special mention for her constant support and understanding when I have disappeared from the family home on various photographic projects or when I have remained busy in my study instead of doing the painting! Lastly, a thanks to my publishers who have allowed me complete freedom to develop this book as I wish.

I hope that you, the reader, enjoy browsing through this book as much as I have enjoyed preparing it.

Michael J Collins,
Colchester.

CHAPTER 1

Historical Background

Railways were founded on the movement of freight. The railway barons of the early 19th century earned vast fortunes from the bulk movement of heavy commodities such as coal, minerals and iron and steel products. Later, when the railways had formed a complete network covering most parts of the country, general merchandise was carried and the railways became the automatic choice of hauliers when speed and reliability was at a premium.

When it was formed, one of the problems which British Railways inherited was the duplication of facilities first set up by the former competing companies. At Peterborough for example, a multiplicity of small freight yards existed – all competing for the same traffic into and out of East Anglia – and far too frequently consignments of freight would be held up while it was shunted from one small yard to another. In the past this debacle had to be tolerated because there simply was no competition from any other mode of transport but, by the early 1950s, a viable road transport system had begun to develop. By the late 1950s it was competing with the railways in a big way. The

A typical fast freight prior to Freightliner launch. Class 40 No.D247 photographed just south of Huntingdon in the early 1960s with the Millerhill-King's Cross goods. Of interest are the small containers which are chained on some of the wagons in the middle of the train. These could hold just four tons of merchandise but were a step in the right direction.

Chris Burton

Two Metrovick Type 2 Co-Bos, Nos D5715 and D5707, provide the power for the "Condor" as it passes Elstree on the 'down' slow line during the late 1950s. This block train of 4-ton containers achieved remarkable timings over the 404 miles between Hendon and Gushetfaulds (Glasgow) via the Settle and Carlisle line and can be regarded as the precursor of the Freightliner concept.

Colin J. Marsden Collection

response by the BR Board was to begin to rationalise its facilities at places like Peterborough and to build new concentrated marshalling yards such as the one in Cambridgeshire at Whitemoor, March, in an attempt to speed up the traffic flow. A fleet of express merchandise freights was also developed such as the famous "Scotch Goods". In 1956 this train left King's Cross yard at 3.15 pm every weekday on a 4 hour 48 minutes non-stop booking to York, Skelton Sidings, and thereafter onwards to Niddrie Yard, Edinburgh, where it arrived in the small hours. Other fast freights were instigated in those last years of steam and, on the whole, they were successful, carrying freight long distances at almost passenger train speeds and at competitive rates.

Whit Saturday 1955 was the day which many regard as the turning point in the haulage of freight by British Railways. The footplatemens' union, ASLEF, went on strike for a 17-day period which reduced all BR services to tatters. This was the first all out stoppage orchestrated by a rail union since the 1926 General Strike and very few trains –

either passenger or freight – were allowed to run. This was a strike of nearly three weeks duration which forced countless regular customers into trying alternative methods of transport. They were there too. The road hauliers had developed lorries which could compete with rail and the emergency arrangements that former BR customers made with the road haulage contractors were all too often seen to be advantageous. Door-to-door service and reliable delivery times are powerful talkers. The whole country was made to see that for delivery of general merchandise it could manage quite well without the railways thank you very much! The loss of this traffic was a severe blow to BR and they tried all that they could to win it back at the cessation of the ASLEF strike. Sadly, however, freight customers left BR in droves, ultimately leaving BR with little else but the bulk haul traffic.

By the late 1950s and early 1960s BR was in the act of reducing intermediate marshalling of trains to try to reduce the time it took to transport goods to its ultimate destination. In order to capitalise on its main advantage over road – the ability to move huge tonnages of merchandise at once – BR was concentrating on gaining the highest possible proportion of block train working and was bidding for trainload traffic. Oil, chemicals, steel, cement, coal, motor car parts and complete vehicles were being moved up and down the country in complete train loads. At the same time

A London-Glasgow Freightliner test train complete with headboard. Headed by Class 40 No.D377, officials climb aboard the locomotive at Willesden sidings in North West London before the train sets off on its 400-mile journey.

Colin J. Marsden Collection

a number of experiments were being conducted to raise the profile of general merchandise traffic by bestowing names on certain services. This was an attempt to woo some of that traffic back from the roads by means of the traffic planners trying to convince customers that their own consignments would receive similar priority to that enjoyed by express trains. One such was the "Condor" which first ran on 16th March 1959 between Hendon and Gushetfaulds in Glasgow. Interestingly, in the context of this book, the train was advertised as carrying 'containers' door-to-door. Not the large containers that we know today, however, but much smaller wooden box-like containers known as IS and BD type containers which were chained down on four-wheel 'Conflat' wagons. They carried just 4 tons of merchandise, usually on pallets. The merchandise which travelled in the train was taken by lorry from the rail heads to the premises of the customer, offering door-to-door service which equalled any road service available at that time. When inaugurated "Condor" was the fastest freight service in Europe, covering the 404 route miles in just under ten hours using a pair of the then new Metrovick Type 2 Co-Bo diesels throughout.

In 1960 the afternoon Tottenham – Whitemoor freight train received the title "Lee Valley Enterprise" and the following fast freight from Chelmsford and Colchester to the Midlands and North received the name "East Essex Enterprise". Both were similar in nature to the original "Condor" service and all could be regarded as the precursor of the

Freightliner trains as we know them today.

In mid 1963 refrigerated containers, known as AF containers, were introduced. These were similar to the boxes used on the "Condor" and other services, but were refrigerated using blocks of dry ice suspended from the ceiling. They were heavily insulated and measured 5 ft 11 in long, 5 ft 5 in wide with a height of 6 ft 3 in. They were used on a number of block trains which BR ran at the time for various ice cream manufacturers and frozen food specialists such as Birds Eye.

The Roadrailer

In 1960 the Freightliner concept as we know it today became closer to reality when the 'Roadrailer' prototype appeared as yet another attempt to thwart road competition. The idea was the brainchild of men working for the US Chesepeake & Ohio Railroad who were looking for an inter-modal freight system which could be used on both road and rail. The vehicle was essentially a conventional road trailer but equipped with alternate road and rail wheel assemblies each fitted with its own braking system. The main selling point was that it required only very basic terminal facilities to change the vehicle from one mode of operation to another. A length of track which was ballasted, concreted or boarded up to rail level was quite sufficient to provide a surface for the road wheels. The only other equipment needed to provide the system was a supply of compressed air to work the wheel raising and lowering apparatus. The idea was first seen in the late 1950s when BR delegates visited the Chesepeake & Ohio and it was they who persuaded the British manufacturers Pressed Steel to obtain a licence to construct the Roadrailer here in the United Kingdom. A full train of the over 50 ft long vehicles was built and it was given protracted trials in late 1961 on the GN and GE lines of the Eastern Region.

Meanwhile, the Beeching Report was published and the

Test train 7Z82 was the first Freightliner to run on the Western Region and it is seen after arrival at Westbury from London on 21st July 1966. Because there was no authority to run without a brake van an air-braked example had to be borrowed from the Southern Region and this can be seen at the rear of the train. What cannot be seen, however, is the branding on the brake van which read "NOT IN COMMON USE To work between Hither Green and Dover only"!

Alec Swain

One of the first Freightliner trains leaves Maiden Lane depot for the long haul up to Glasgow behind Brush Type 4 No. D1837 during 1965. Note the guard's caboose placed on the leading wagon immediately behind the locomotive.

International Standards Organisation (ISO) container was put forward as the only valid inter-modal transportation system which had any chance at all of winning back the lost mercandise freight traffic. The days of the Roadrailer were thus numbered before they had really begun and two years were allowed to elapse – albeit with occasional trial runs of the train – before an announcement that a London – Newcastle – Edinburgh service would be instigated in August 1963. As fate would have it, the experimental train broke a coupling whilst on a proving trial on the East Coast Main Line just a few days before its scheduled launch date and the start of the service was postponed. The defect was rectified by Pressed Steel and the complete train of Roadrailer vehicles was accepted by BR during the 1963-64 winter.

At headquarters level the Roadrailer supporters were fighting for a radical commercial stance. This was because they were attracting little or no business with projected tariffs based on BR freight charging principles which were years out of date. They felt that the brand new inter-modal technique should boast an imaginative pricing policy designed to make the most of the strengths of the system. In retrospect, it can be seen that what they were really pursuing was the arrangement imposed on the BRB some years later when Freightliners were transferred to the aegis of the National Freight Corporation. The idea that they were pursuing was that customers should own, hire or lease their own Roadrailer units and that BR should only charge a fare for the trunk haul part of the journey. In 1964, they won this battle but only by forming a separate company – British Roadrailer Services – which was set as a subsidiary of the BRB and the Transport holding company which existed at that time. In essence, it was the same pattern that was set up for the activities of Freightliners after the 1968 Transport Act.

It is sad to record here that British Roadrailers never ever turned a wheel in revenue earning service. Doubly sad, because in retrospect the system had much to recommend it. It can be argued that the simplicity of the system, without the costly adherence to expensive terminal facilities, could well have won back a good deal of the merchandise traffic which to this day eludes Freightliners.

The Liner Train is Born

Although there had been flirtations by BR in carrying containers in normal freight trains before, it was not until 1963 that BR began to have serious thoughts on the subject of running complete train loads of containers at express passenger speeds. It was reported in the October 1964 railway periodicals that construction of equipment for the first Liner Train prototype had begun – the vehicles at Shildon and the fibreglass containers at Eastleigh. Meanwhile, Dr Beeching had stated that the first services should be running by the end of 1964. By contrast, the BR industrial magazine *Transport Age* was less optimistic. It acknowledged that the liner train was the 'linchpin' of future merchandise freight services for BR. It tempered this remark by finding rather a damper however; the vast capital sums needed to produce the road/rail transfer terminals in an integrated network.

Then came the inevitable union problems. The National Union of Railwaymen (NUR) opposed the liner trains because private road hauliers would be allowed to collect and deliver goods at the rail terminals. They found this position absolutely untenable. Negotiations between the NUR and BR reached a compromise however, and during the summer and early autumn of 1965 full scale trial runs were conducted with liner trains equipped with empty boxes. Another point of contention at this time was the

Close-up of the guard's caboose which was used on early Freightliner trains but was an absolute disaster because wagon suspension is not designed for the comfort of people. After languishing for twenty years at Stratford depot it was handed over to the National Railway Museum. Note the round cupola used by guards to keep a look out when the train was in motion.
National Railway Museum

question of where the guards were going to ride on the new trains. The original intention was for guards to travel in the rear cab of the locomotive but the rail unions were adamant that this was not going to be the case. During the spring and summer of 1965 the BR board entered into protracted negotiations with the unions but were forced to concede the point.

Early Freightliner trains ran with a passenger guards van coupled behind the engine and some ran with a freight guards van coupled conventionally at the rear of the train. An interesting experiment occurred when a 10 ft container of 485 cubic ft capacity was adapted and made into a guard's brake or caboose. It was fitted with a door, window cupola and a telephone link with the locomotive crew. A propane gas supply was bolted to the outside of the container for heating and lighting. A number of runs were made with this contraption forming the last container on the train. The ride given to the guard however, was diabolical

because Freightliner flats were not sprung with passenger comfort in mind. More than a few guards indeed, had a nightmare ride and ended up being flung across the container and injured when traversing sharp curves or junctions at speed. Ventilation was provided by two aluminium sliding grilles which, when opened at 70 mph, subjected the guard to a howling gale! The sole example languished at Stratford for nearly twenty years but on 7th October 1985 it was handed over to the National Railway Museum at York. On handing over the caboose, Mr Bryan Driver, Chairman and Managing Director of Freightliners Ltd, described it as "an unmitigated disaster". The demise of the caboose, however, resulted in the guards travelling in the rear cab of the locomotive – just as BR had originally intended!

The date of 15th November 1965 is highly significant in this story because on that date the first trial liner trains carrying revenue earning payloads were allowed to run. Right until a few hours before their scheduled departure time the train's running was in doubt because of the union's stance. Mr Sidney Green, the union's general secretary, urged his members to co-operate and a promise by the Railways Board that only railway hauliers would be allowed to operate at the terminals for the trial runs led to union backing for the trials.

At 20.05 therefore, one train left North London's Maiden

Lane terminal for the 400 mile run to Glasgow (Gushetfaulds) and at 20.17 another train left Glasgow on the southbound haul. There were 13 Freightliner wagons carrying 39 containers on the train which left London, together with a dynamometer car for testing purposes. What is not generally known is that only three containers carried a commercial load, the others were either empty or carried lengths of old rail for ballast to simulate commercial loads. The commercial traffic was 15 tons of confectionery, six tons of foodstuffs and five tons of metals. The southbound train hauled 34 containers of which only three held a revenue earning payload of beer, firebricks and paper. Freightliner

was launched however, and between 1964 and 1969 the UK government spent over £25 million developing the system – a fortune indeed at this period. With such a commitment it was inevitable that Freightliner was to blossom and develop.

A Freightliner train in 1965 sweeps down the electrified West Coast Main Line near Watford behind a Class 47 diesel. Note the air-braked brake van bringing up the rear – an expedient used for some time following the disastrous caboose experiment and prior to guard's agreeing to ride in the rear cab of the locomotive.

Chapter 2

Freightliner Profile

Organisation

As outlined in the previous chapter, the original development of the Freightliner concept was made by British Railways and operations began, on one route only, from November 1965. Under the provisions of the 1968 Transport Act, the enterprise was vested in a new company, Freightliner Limited, which was placed under the control of the newly-formed National Freight Corporation (NFC). Under NFC management Freightliner grew to become the world's largest overland container haulier.

The 1976 Transport Act transferred Freightliner Ltd back to the British Railways Board as a wholly owned, separately accountable subsidiary company within the rail freight portfolio. In 1988 came another change because in October of that year Freightliner merged with Railfreight Ltd. Previously, Freightliner had functioned independently of the main Railfreight business, but BR wanted to bring all non bulk traffic flows under one umbrella. The impetus for the merger came partly from the very real prospect of additional business after the Channel Tunnel is opened in 1993. It was desired that no longer should Railfreight and Freightliner be competing for the same business but, instead, the combined organisation, to be known as Railfreight Distribution, would be able to offer the customer whichever system was best suited to his individual requirements. One consequence of this merger was the joint operation of certain train services. Hardly had the new arrangements been announced, when a new train link between Bristol and Coatbridge (Glasgow) was established, conveying Freightliner wagons in a scheduled Speedlink service for part of the journey.

Early Days

Prior to the formation of Freightliner, BR was losing freight at the rate of over 3% a year, and in a vast modernisation plan of the 1950s had underestimated and miscalculated the depth of the growing competition from the lorry. The new railway wagons which the planners had designed were far too slow, being restricted to vacuum braking, and the system of marshalling wagons and forwarding them was both cumbersome and rough. The road haulage competitors were succeeding in getting the goods to the customer's door often on the same day that they were despatched, whilst the railways were still marshalling their wagons and often succeeding in damaging the goods.

Two important points need to be emphasised in the process of understanding the planning decisions made by the early Freightliner engineers. First, although certain shipping companies were at the same time launching the deep sea container revolution, British Rail was concentrating, quite independently, on the merits of containerisation with the needs of the domestic market in mind. There were, at that time, no standard container sizes and there was certainly no standard equipment for handling containers. Secondly, Britain's railway gauge was diminutive when compared with the more generous loading gauges available to Continental and American railways. This made the BR network unsuited to the trailer or flatcar concept; the piggyback or kangaroo systems which were then in vogue in other parts of the world. Early designs therefore, called for a low platform wagon to accommodate the 8 ft high boxes considered to be the minimum viable size, with a wheel diameter size not exceeding 2 ft 8 in. The goal was 75mph running and an axle loading of 17.5 tonnes, since increased to 20 tonnes. The bigger boxes are now 8 ft 6in tall and BR has spent millions of pounds extending clearances on its Freightliner network to accommodate the new size container.

The early criteria called for a specification of a 60 ft wagon with air brakes. A rigid draw bar coupling system was incorporated to avoid jolting and bumping of the wagons during rapid changes in speed. This ensured that the customer would be able to reduce packaging levels to the levels enjoyed when transporting their goods by road.

Too big for the British loading gauge is the 'kangaroo' or 'piggy back' sytem where lorry trailer units are put on the train for the trunk haul. It is not so in the USA, however, where Santa Fe diesels Nos 3438, 3424 and 3416 were recorded taking a northbound trailer train over the Colorado Joint Line at Palmer Lake on 30th September 1988.

Kim Fullbrook

Handling equipment was more difficult to produce. Planners, engineers and operators searched the world for industrially proven equipment which could be adapted to the criteria designated by Freightliner. Such equipment had to be speedy, versatile, extremely reliable and capable of continuous operation night and day in most weather conditions. Portal and gantry cranes of various shapes and sizes, conveyor systems, and side, front and horizontal transfer equipment were among the hardware considered for use.

The initial choice was a portal crane spanning both road and rail tracks; the Drott Travelift, developed over several years in the United States. It was equipped with a grappler frame whose legs were able to lift containers between ten and thirty feet in length by means of lift pockets at the bottom. These machines were diesel powered, worked by hydraulics and mounted on pneumatic tyres. They could therefore be temporarilly moved to another part of the yard for maintenance – a benefit lost on subsequent purchases of bigger cranes. Fourteen Travelifts were acquired and gave sterling service for a few years.

From 1966, the newer 8 ft 6 in ISO standard maritime containers began to appear in the system and it became apparent that the choice of the 8 ft square profile container for the early Freightliner boxes would have to be altered. Despite this, Freightliner in order to meet the domestic road competition, still had to retain bottom lift (as opposed to corner lift on the ISO boxes) as a means of handling flats of up to 8 ft 6 in width for the home market.

By this time the Travelift, not designed for continuous working was showing its limitations and causing problems. Traffic had expanded from 27,000 containers per annum in 1966 to 400,000 containers per annum three years later. The machines simply could not cope with the demands of this level of operation with intensive use round the clock. The solution adopted was an electric rail-mounted crane, still of the Portal type, but built by Herbert Morris of Loughborough. Some thirty machines were ordered by Freightliner and many of them are in use today.

Marketing

Although Freightliner enjoyed the benefits of rapid expansion and early success in attracting traffic, by the late 1960s it was suffering severe losses. At this time the company reorganised its marketing on product lines which comprised the three principal sectors of the business: Irish and Home Trade, Deep Sea and European. The reason for this was that Freightliner wanted to see themselves as a more professional outfit, one that could react quickly to opportunities in individual market sectors. In addition they wanted to examine the costs and performances of individual routes in much greater detail. It was recognised that the main overheads were terminal costs and the contract payments to BR for running the trains. The latter were fairly fixed. They could not, therefore afford to run services which did not show a profit.

Freightliner was originally conceived as a haulier of goods for the home trade but today this accounts for less than half of the business. This is the result of changing patterns of industry within the UK. Heavy industry and manufacturing in city centres has declined considerably. In addition, important changes in retailing have taken place over the last twenty years or so, hand in hand with the development of supermarket shopping etc. Many of Freightliner's original customers were forced to move away from rail transport in favour of using the motorway system under the influence of commercial pressures.

In the late 1970s casual haulage, dependant on parcels and steel, suffered a general decline. Throughout the entire haulage industry there was a tendency to move towards greater specialisation and to develop longer term haulage commitments from customers. Freightliner was no exception and in addition they made a decision to move up market in order to attract greater revenue. They tried to concentrate on what they considered they did best and to maximise reward. That meant pursuing longer distance movements and searching for higher value cargoes. This is where the premiums of security, reliability and safety, which Freightliner could easily offer were most valued. They were successful in attracting this custom and end of year profits gradually improved.

Trade with Ireland presented Freightliner with several unique problems. The structure of the trade changed rapidly in the late 1970s and early 1980s because of the industrial depression in the North coupled with Eire's burgeoning trade within the EEC. To compound problems, competition was heightened when P&O launched a rival service in 1975. In order to bolster its position, Freightliner successfully persuaded a number of deep sea shipping lines to serve Ireland through English ports via the Freightliner network, rather

Success story of the last fifteen years has been the 45% market share attained by Freightliner in the deep sea container trade. Class 40 No. 40057 passes Doncaster station on 30th June 1984 with a well loaded special Freightliner from Felixstowe.

Michael J. Collins

than having the additional expense of using a feeder ship. A considerable proportion of the business to the south of Ireland is this deep sea traffic and it keeps the terminal at Holyhead very active.

There is no doubt however, that Freightliner's biggest success in recent times has been deep sea traffic. Indicative of this success is the fact that at the present time over 45% of all deep sea containers arriving at UK ports use the Freightliner system. The container revolution of the last twenty years or so has projected Freightliner into the natural role as the land link of the deep sea container lines. It is the additional facilities which Freightliner can offer shippers which enables it to attract so much of this trade. Rail haul, collection and delivery, storage, box repair, cleaning and control are extras which make Freightliner an attractive proposition to shippers, and because their service is precise and reliable, shipowners can improve ship turnround. This enables them in turn, to offer a better service to their own customers. The success of this package enables Freightliner to boast that it carries well over half of the boxes moved from Southampton – one of the UK's biggest and busiest container ports. The ports of Tilbury and Felixstowe have become increasingly dominant in the deep sea trade and both are well served by direct Freightliner services. For deep sea shipping lines calling at ports further north, there are direct rail facilities into the container berths at Seaforth (Liverpool). Also, where rail facilities exist at smaller ports such as Grangemouth and Newhaven special services have been provided according to the dictates of customer demand.

European marketing and trade is not quite so easy because the comparatively shorter sea crossings enables the roll-on roll-off ferry operators to offer a competitive package. Another factor of course, has been the fact that many European railways have been slow in the past at developing a comprehensive container train network. Recent developments within the EEC however, have been helpful to Freightliner. A growth in restrictive traffic regulations aimed at the heavy freight haulage sector, ranging from driver's hours limitations to even a complete ban on lorry movements at weekends has put up hauliers' costs. The Channel Tunnel will also make it easier for Freightliner to compete, as long through journeys from the UK to southern Europe without handling at UK ports will be possible.

Until the end of 1982 the Freightliner role in European trade was that of sub-contractor in the UK to and from ports for other well established European container operators. In January 1983, Freightliner became responsible for the container shipping service between Harwich and Zeebrugge. The decision was taken that Freightliner, in its own right, should enter the European market.

Pricing and Marketing

When Freightliner was formed a completely new price structure was devised. This was a completely new tariff based only on the size of the container and the route. There was no directional pricing, nor differentials depending on the nature of the goods being carried, but a discount incentive scheme was adopted. The basic charge was calculated so that prices were below road haulage rates. When the new prices were announced a Sunday newspaper implied that Freightliner rates had been pitched at almost 'loss

Deep sea traffic passing Purfleet on 29th June 1989 in the form of Class 86 No. 86427 heading the 13.58 Tilbury-Garston Freightliner. Class 86s had gained access to the LTS lines the previous year when the North London Line was electrified through to Stratford.

Ken Brunt

leader' rates to net the first customers. This was absolutely false because Freightliner was researched and designed to be an integral part of the modern industrial process. Study of the market, scale of flows and the form they took pointed to the container as the tool that could be best integrated with the modern industrial process. Freightliner had to win business on terms that justified the heavy investment that had been placed in it if the network was to develop. Studies of road transport costs, performance and rates had been undertaken before Freightliner rates were decided and fixed. Road transport rates were not to be undercut at all costs – a price war would have done nobody any good.

Selective pricing was applied to Freightliner traffic from 1st December 1968. 'Direction differentials' were introduced on a number of routes where the balance of tonnage each way was uneven. This was done to give traders themselves an incentive to organise a return load. Thus, for example, it cost £14 to send a 20 ft box from Manchester to Cardiff as against £16 in the reverse direction. Other routes on which these differentials applied included Sheffield to Glasgow, Sheffield to London and Cardiff to Glasgow. Freightliner was very succesful in attracting traffic and soon was

carrying nearly 500,000 TEUs (Twenty ft Equivalent Units) per annum. Although some road hauliers were beginning to use Freightliner, many viewed the new organisation as direct competitors however and there was a distinct reluctance to place traffic on the rails for fear that they may try to poach traffic. It was partly to overcome this fear that ownership of Freightliner was transferred, in 1969, from the BRB to a newly formed state owned road haulage corporation called the National Freight Corporation (NFC).

Freightliner became an independent limited company and, for the first time, separate trading accounts had to be issued. These showed the company to be losing over £2 million on a revenue of £10.8 million. This situation was quite unacceptable to the NFC which had a remit from the government to make profits. The Freightliner marketing policy was put into question and the cheaper-than-road tarriff abandoned. Prices were increased above the rate of inflation by over 10% between 1969 and 1971. The consequence of this was a flattening out of business for a time, but by 1971 increased deep sea trade enabled Freightliner to record its first profit. The company has achieved profits in nearly every year since 1971.

Freightliner has to be able to react quickly to market forces. An illustration of this ability occurred in 1981 when Freightliner perceived a short term market for carrying sawdust from Great Yarmouth to Coatbridge. The material was loaded into containers at Great Yarmouth and sent down to Ipswich in a special train to connect with the regular overnight Felixstowe to Coatbridge train. Class 31 No. 31243 passes Haughley Junction with the 12.16 special 'Sawdustliner' from Great Yarmouth to Coatbridge on 5th June 1981.

John C. Baker

Sometimes traffic becomes available at ports where no Freightliner terminal facilities exist and special arrangements have to be made for the unloading of containers. This was the case on 26th August 1983 when Class 33 No. 33060 passed Newhaven Town with a special Freightliner for Newhaven Harbour.

Paul D. Shannon

What makes Freightliner unique amongst other transport operators is the ability to use rail for the trunk haul portion of the journey. The cost of railway movements has never been perceived as an exact science, though the recent sectorisation of British Rail is beginning to concentrate minds. One of the major problems is that many joint facilities are used in the course of a journey by a train of almost any sector. Railway track and signalling will be used for example, by trains of many different sectors in any particular day. Freightliner, however, has for a long time had a clear indication of its rail trunking costs because it has had to pay BR the calculated cost of running its block trains. These costs have revealed some very similar characteristics to road costs. The first is that rail costs vary very little according to the size of the load being trunked. It costs much the same to move ten wagons carrying 30 TEUs as it does to move a 20 wagon train carrying 60 TEUs. Freightliner design their plan therefore, to include as many 20-wagon trains as possible. The costs do vary by distance and there is a strong linear relationship. The fact is though, that rail trunk haul costs less than a quarter of the same distance by road. This begs a question: why is it that not all goods are trunked by rail? The reason is quite straight forward. In order to use rail the container has to be brought up to the rail terminal by road and once at the terminal has to be transferred between road and rail. The cost of carrying out these activities can be high and are incurred no matter how far the container has to be transported. Unfortunately, the economics of rail trunk haul are not seen to the full in short distances.

Road collection and delivery costs can in fact, be the major element in the total cost of using the Freightliner system. These costs vary in a direct relationship to how far the customer is away from the Freightliner terminal and so the exact siting of the terminal is a crucial decision. Clearly, it is this relationship which often allows Freightliner to score when handling deep sea cargoes. The terminal is situated right in the docks and containers can be loaded almost directly from the ship onto the Freightliner wagon. The cost of getting the goods to the terminal is effectively ruled out and customers can gain from the cheap rate that BR can offer for the trunk haul element.

Freightliner are essentially full-load carriers, the unit of load being the container which is loaded and unloaded on the customers' own premises. Once loaded, the container remains a secure package until it reaches its destination which might entail several modes of travel. In effect the container acts as a pipeline between firms, it has the added advantage of being flexible and traffic can be directed to all parts of the countrywide network as requirements dictate. It is this extreme flexibility of the bi-modal system which Freightliner pushes in its present day marketing strategies.

The basis of prices quoted for the carriage of containers today by Freightliner is according to type, size and ownership of the container whatever it contains. Customers are constantly reminded to keep within stipulated payloads because overloading could easily violate road traffic statutory requirements. Spot checks are often made on a random basis at a public weighbridge.

Freightliner do not publish a standard tariff and customers are quoted prices which reflects the competitive market situation in relation to the route concerned. Rates quoted will vary according to the value of the customer's business with the company, the amount of balanced working and its regularity. Prices quoted might be for trunk movement only from terminal to terminal or be inclusive of road collection and delivery. In the case of very large businesses, package deals are sought and service and pricing are the subject of contractual arrangements.

Closed Terminals

Class 47 No.47380 prepares to leave Follingsby Freightliner Terminal, Newcastle-upon-Tyne, on 30th March 1987 with the evening train to Cardiff. The terminal closed a week later on 6th April 1987.

Ian S. Carr

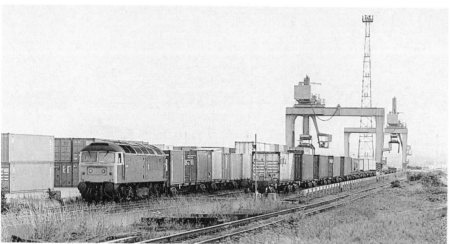

Stockton container terminal closed in February 1989 when it was replaced by more modern facilities at the new Cleveland Terminal at nearby Wilton. In happier times Class 47 No. 47196 prepares to leave with the 18.05 departure to Darlington on 16th July 1986.

Paul D. Shannon

A victim of the Freightliner profitability drive of the mid-1980s was Dudley Terminal, West Midlands. The rather cramped layout of this terminal is evident as Class 45 'Peak' No. 45003 leaves the terminal on 19th April 1984 with the 18.45 departure to Glasgow. The train will combine with a departure from Lawley Street at Bescot Yard and will continue the overnight haul to Scotland with electric traction.

Geoff Dowling

Class 20s are most unusual traction for Freightliner trains but the photographer was lucky enough to record a pair in action at the now-closed Clydeport Terminal at Greenock on 5th July 1986. Nos 20228 and 20192 have just brought in the daily 'Hapag Lloyd' company container train.

George C. O'Hara

Edinburgh Freightliner Terminal was situated on the site of the one-time Portobello engineer's yard. It was closed from 6th April 1987 along with eight other terminals. On 16th June 1983 Class 40 No. 40057 was recorded leaving with the 19.30 service to King's Cross.

Bert Wynn

Closures

Freightliner has to be adept at reacting to market forces and over the last 25 years a number of terminals have been closed as a result of economies forced by changing patterns of trade. An early casualty for example, was the terminal at Sheffield which was sadly affected by the decline of the stainless steel making and finishing industry within the city.

In January 1987 it was announced that eight more depots were to be closed effective from 6th April 1987. Aberdeen, Dundee, Edinburgh, Newcastle, Hull, Manchester Longsight, Swansea and Nottingham terminals were all shed from the network. This was part of a reorganisation of Freightliner marketing and operations into just two business units – Deep Sea and European. The latter unit was to deal with the home market and Irish trade in addition to European markets. A total of 480 jobs were lost in the restructuring including 80 at the London headquarters. The rationale behind the closures was the continued search for profitability. At the time Freightliner were charged by the government to meet a target of 6% return on capital by 1991-92. In the 1985/86 trading year the company only returned a trading profit of £94,000 on a turnover of £106.9 million.

One of the aims of the restructuring was to concentrate on the long haul business – by that time quoted as over 400 km. Freightliner were also keen to concentrate on maritime trade which, by that time, made up over half of its traffic. It was ironic that Aberdeen still had to be chopped out despite generating 65% of its traffic for Willesden – twice the minimum long haul distance and the longest single route on the entire system! It is also interesting to dwell on the apparent increase in rail's 'long haul' distance thresholds over the passing years. In the 1960s pundits considered that a distance of over 150-200 miles, rail had the edge. This made traffic between many industrial and population centres in England and Wales as well as Anglo-Scottish traffic a viable proposition. This erosion of rail's competitive edge reflects the major advances which have taken place in road haulage competitiveness as the motorway and major road network has been improved. Maximum vehicle weights and sizes too, have increased over the years and road haulage companies have been able to respond to market forces.

In the 1980s Freightliner adopted new forms of marketing in order to face up to the more challenging business climate of the time. Manufacturers have, when faced with the increasingly complex nature of transport and distribution, tried to handover all of their problems to another organisation. In other words distribution has been more and more sub contracted to specialists. Road hauliers have not been slow to respond to this challenge and Freightliner have also entered into this arena with 'Freightpoint', which offers additional services such as inventory control, warehousing and break-bulk facilities. In the first Freightpoint operation Freightliner teamed up with the Falkirk based road haulage outfit James Kelman to transport and distribute whisky from Scotland to the South East. Wines and spirits were organised to come up in the reverse direction. James Kelman had the bonded warehouse facilities and was in charge of the road distribution, whilst obviously, Freightliner provided the trunk haul part of the deal.

Problems

One of the major problems of railway container operations is that of meeting customer requirements. Failure to do this can result in a quick loss of business. There are real difficulties encountered in changing the Freightliner product. Many customers for example, demand pallet, side-loading of open platform containers with curtain sides. Road wagons can easily cope with 40 ft containers which will accommodate two 4 ft pallets loaded side by side. The 40 ft container with curtain sides is difficult to adapt to rail transit because of a lack of rigidity. Bagged powder products such as milk and fertilizer settle in transit and become out of gauge as the bags bulge at the sides. It is difficult then, in addition, to use bottom-loading equipment since the grab arms fall foul of the bulging sides of the load. The rigid box deep sea traffic does not give these problems but more and more shippers are switching to containers which are 9 ft high and these cannot be accommodated in the British loading gauge using the current wagons. A new build of wagons using smaller diameter wheels, so that the larger containers can be transported, is now being evaluated. A prototype was exhibited in Spring 1989 at a Railfreight exhibition at Cricklewood.

A major problem is that of wear and tear on resources. This book marks the 25th anniversary of the running of the first services and the fact is that much of the equipment in use today is also of that age. The wagons themselves have been worked to death, averaging over 70,000 miles a year at speeds of up to 75 mph. As much as 120,000 miles a year is being achieved from sets of stock on the more demanding diagrams. The wagons have had a strenuous working life, being intensively diagrammed with long stretches of running at speed. In addition, in a move aimed at keeping Freightliner ahead of increasing lorry tare weights, the wagons are now passed to carry 62 tonnes – 10 tonnes more than their design weight. Careful maintenance work by the engineers have lifted their availability to well over 85% in recent years but many are now becoming life expired and are beginning to be troublesome. The strain of the everyday hammering the veteran flats are receiving is showing up in problems with the axlebox bearings and the connecting pins between wagons. The wagons are permanently coupled in rakes of five and it can be a major operating problem if one wagon in the set is declared unfit to run through some defect. It can lead to four others stranded in a very inconvenient part of the system until a suitable replacement can be found and brought up with a match wagon to the place in question.

On 18th May 1990 the Secretary of State for Transport approved Railfreight Distribution's plans to build 700 new wagons for use on its maritime services. At an initial cost of £40 million it is the largest order for rail freight wagons placed by the BR Board for over a decade.

Series production is destined to commence in 1991 at an initial build rate of five wagons a week. They will replace 760 wagons which are stated to be "life expired". In all 560 outer wagons and 140 inner wagons are to be constructed. This will allow an equal number of sets of two and three wagons to be operated. This expedient will allow more flexibility in adjusting train lengths according to the dictates of traffic demand.

Cranes at the terminals are also becoming old in some cases. There have been renewals in the past but modern Freightliner thinking is that two medium-size cranes in a terminal are more efficient. This is because they make the terminal less prone to congestion and ensures cover in the event of crane failure. All this is going to require investment by Railfreight Distribution on a quite massive scale in the next few years.

Chapter 3

Network and Services

Network Build Up

Success was claimed almost immediately for Freightliner. After two weeks of largely experimental running following the first train on 15th November 1965 from London to Glasgow, the trains were described as running with "absolute reliability". Strangely, November 1965 was remarkable for Arctic type weather in the British Isles and while the roads over Shap were blocked leaving road vehicles stranded the Freightliners were achieving record runs! One train reached the Glasgow depot at Gushetfaulds 51 minutes ahead of schedule, having covered the 391 miles at an average speed of 51 mph. Other liner trains had arrived early and had thus achieved the objective of having all containers transported overnight available to customers by 6 am daily. Deliveries to final destinations had been to the exact times asked by customers. All users of the system were expressing total satisfaction. The figures for the number of containers carried at this time are interesting. During the fortnight's running from 15th November there were just 30 containers of commercial traffic in the first week and 41 in the second. Goods carried included televisions, electric cookers, washing machines, chocolate, cereals and canned beer.

From the small beginning made in November 1965 the Freightliner network was quickly expanded. Bearing in mind that Freightliner was originally conceived as serving the inland market, the entire network was almost complete five years later, following millions of pounds of government investment. By 1969 Freightliner were beginning to see the start of deep sea containerisation in the UK. This market was an obvious one for Freightliner to bid for, particularly the inland movement of containers and they quickly developed close working relationships with the emerging container shipping lines. They succeeded in capturing at the outset a large market share. This allowed them to increase carryings and by 1971 they were moving nearly 100,000 TEUs of deep sea traffic. This business, together with higher prices then being charged for the domestic business, enabled Freightliner to record their first profit in 1971 and a new era of expansion was under way.

During the 1970s therefore, Freightliner built new terminals at all the major ports and inland customs clearance depots and invested through British Rail in clearing the railway gauge on major routes for 8 ft 6 in containers following the change in the ISO standard. Now Freightliner operates between 23 depots throughout the UK plus Dublin in the Republic of Ireland. Over 100 services are run every weekday and they link all the country's major industrial centres and container ports.

Following the running of the very first Freightliner train, operations were quickly built up and six nightly services were operating by early 1966. On 31st October of the same year the first Freightliner train to use the East Coast Main Line (ECML) was run. This was the 18.35 King's Cross-Aberdeen and the 11.50 in the reverse direction. Within a year there was a Sheffield service to and from Stratford gaining the ECML at Finsbury Park and on 8th May 1967 a third London-Glasgow service started running between King's Cross and Gushetfaulds, again via the ECML. The London Midland Region introduced a container service between London and Belfast on 3rd April 1967. A special train was run using Freightliner containers and wagons via a scheduled ordinary freight service from Camden Freight Terminal to Heysham. The train connected with a time-tabled container vessel at Heysham. Containers were delivered to any destination in Ulster the next day. Later, on 5th June 1967, a King's Cross-Felixstowe train was inaugurated for crew training purposes with the real thing following some weeks later. The first terminal in Wales, at Cardiff was opened by The Rt Hon. Barbara Castle MP, then Minister of Transport on 8th June 1967.

In August 1967 a boost to the company's image was gratefully received when the Royal Family and staff decided to move their luggage and office equipment to Balmoral

The first of BR's cellular ships, especially designed for shipment of containers on the Zeebrugge route was christened *Sea Freightliner I* and is seen at Harwich Parkeston Quay being unloaded. Note the giant Stothert & Pitt 30-ton crane behind, which will load containers straight onto trains for onward delivery.

The second of BR's purpose-built container ships, *Sea Freightliner II* approaches Parkeston Quay on 1st June 1970. Note the containers stacked on the deck and the 'Sealink' ferry departing in the background.

by Freightliner. All property was loaded aboard a single container and sent from King's Cross to Aberdeen. Later in August of the same year the South Wales-London steel Freightliner carried a record 700 tons of steel. This was in a capacity load of 53 containers, 24 destined for Fords of Dagenham, nine more for Vauxhall of Luton and the balance for various customers in London and the South East.

Another benchmark in the story of Freightliner occurred on 2nd December 1967 when the first of two cellular 4,000-ton container ships built by John Redhead & Sons Ltd was launched at South Shields. Christened *Sea Freightliner I* it was due to commence work on high capacity sea container services between Harwich and Zeebrugge the following year. The first BR high capacity direct container service between England and Holland was opened on 18th June 1968 when *Sea Freightliner I* left Harwich at 04.45 for Princes Margrithaven, Rotterdam. A second ship for the Holland service, *Sea Freightliner II*, was launched at the same shipyard on 15th March 1968. On 1st January 1968 a direct high capacity container service between London, the West Midlands and the Republic of Ireland began via Holyhead and Dublin. The LMR's ship *MV Harrogate* was converted to carry 28 containers per voyage between Holyhead and Dun Laoghaire. Later the same month the first terminal on the Southern Region and the first of BR's Stage II Freightliner terminals started operation when Southampton despatched its first train to Stratford Terminal. At Stratford this train connected with the Stockton train and itself formed the Stratford to Leeds working the same night – thus offering a through Southampton-Leeds service overnight. The Fyffes Banana Company was an early user of this train. On 5th February 1968 Southampton launched its second service which was destined for the West Midlands terminal at Dudley. This train set was used for the Dudley-Newcastle working the same night giving Southampton direct links with the far North East. The new terminal at Southampton was built on the former Millbrook goods yard site and took this name when a second (Maritime) terminal was opened later.

London-Paris

In order to train crews, Freightliner test running took place in early 1968 between London (Stewarts Lane) and places in Kent such as Ramsgate and Margate. This allowed a real landmark in the growth of the network to occur on 22nd April 1968 when, as a joint venture between BR and SNCF, the direct London-Paris Freightliner was launched. The first train was flagged away from Stratford Terminal behind Class 47 No. D1758. The train ran via the Dover-Dunkirk train ferry and had departures from both capitals five days a week

without any major expenditure on fixed installations or ships. This train consisted of up to 14 BR Freightliner wagons which had been specially modified for ferry conveyance and for running in France. It had a capacity of 42 ISO 20 ft containers. Special arrangements had to be made so that the train could be accommodated on the four tracks of the ferry vessels. Instead of running in the customary five-wagon sets the train was made up of two four-wagon sets and two three-wagon sets. On arrival at the port the train could be split so that the four-wagon sets could be parked on the centre tracks of the vessel which was slightly

A modern container vessel unloading containers at the Port of Felixstowe.

Photographs of the Par-Park Royal Freightliner are very rare but this one has come to light of Class 47 No. D1675 *Amazon* (now withdrawn) passing Dawlish Warren with the train on 3rd June 1969, about three weeks after the train was first run.

Terry Nichols

longer. The train left Stratford at 12.55, the relatively early departure time was chosen to obviate the need for a freight conflicting with peak rush hour services on the Southern Region.

A strange feature of this working was that, unlike other Freightliner services, the formation of the wagons was not fixed. The London-Paris train imposed an additional demand for limited shipping space on vessels which also carry the normal train ferry and roll-on/roll-off traffic. The Paris Freightliner was therefore, not run as a fixed formation but the length of the train was adjusted from day to day according to the dictates of the demand for space. Although the length of the train varied from day to day, the same number of wagons normally left both London and Paris on any individual day in an effort to ensure a balance of rolling stock at each end. The two terminals would assess the size of the train required to be run the following day taking into account such factors as space reservations already made.

Stratford and Paris would liaise by Telex and the terminal with the heavier demand for wagons would determine the length of the train in both directions. Table 1 shows the timetable used for the London-Paris Freightliner operations.

Table 1
London-Paris Freightliner Timetable

OUTWARD			INWARD
12.55 Dep.	London (Stratford F.L. Terminal)		Arr. 08.00
16.28 Arr.	Dover		Dep. 04.50
17.30 Dep.	Dover		Arr. 03.30
21.15 Arr.	Dunkirk		Dep. 22.45
21.22 Dep.	Dunkirk		Arr. 21.50
02.58 Arr.	Paris (La Chappelle-Annexe)		Dep. 17.50

The Saturday morning Ripple Lane (Barking)-Southampton (Maritime) Freightliner has to traverse the web of lines in North London before it joins the West of England main line at Acton Wells Junction for the journey down to the coast via Reading and Basingstoke. Class 47 No.47050 threads the North London Line between Kensall Rise and Willesden with this train on 5th March 1983.

Michael J. Collins

The two capital cities are the focus of the rail systems in their respective countries. Most traffic was exchanged between the two metropolitan districts but there was considerable scope for transfer of traffic to the provincial and commercial areas – in France by means of conventional express freight trains. The London-Paris tariff offered highly competitive rates on a 'per container' basis in relation to that offered by road haulage companies. Charges were the same whether the container was full or returning back empty. The train was diagrammed for Southern Region haulage from 6th May 1969 but by Summer 1969 loadings were very poor and comments in the press indicated that the amount of boxes being handled barely justified its existence. Unfortunately the London-Paris service was discontinued in Summer 1970.

Further Growth

In April 1968 livestock was transported for the first time by Freightliner when a trial consignment of 48 Hereford cross and pure Friesian calves were taken from Longcross, Surrey, to Huntley, Aberdeenshire. They travelled in specially constructed open cartons within curtain-sided Type M containers on the King's Cross-Aberdeen freightliner.

On 20th May 1968 the Par-Park Royal (West London) Freightliner was inaugurated when Class 47 No. D1641 hauled the first train eastwards. The containers were loaded at Par by a 30-ton crawler crane on hire to BR. One of the biggest customers was English China Clays Ltd (ECC) who ordered a number of tippable containers especially for the traffic. They were used in an experimental delivery service of china clay from the ECC plant at Par to the Croxley paper mill of John Dickenson & Company near Watford. Each container carried a load of 15 tons of china clay and had a loaded gross weight of 16 tons. The sheeted containers were despatched each afternoon in the regular Freightliner train to Park Royal where they were distributed by road to Croxley. On 11th November 1968 Plymouth became connected to the Freightliner network, when the Divisional Manager flagged off the 16.35 from Friary. This service was a portion of the Par-Park Royal train which was retimed to leave Par at 15.15 and, after picking up the Friary portion, left Plymouth at 17.00 arriving in London at 21.52. Unfortunately, services on the Par-Plymouth-London Freightliner ceased in mid 1970 because of unsatisfactory patronage in both directions. The space released at Park Royal (itself now closed) was used to step up capacity on the South Wales-London steel Freightliners running at this time. Plymouth still sees very occasional Freightliner trains, however, running as specials for the various military establishments in the area.

By the end of May 1968 BR's weekly container loadings passed the 5,000 mark for the first time, and in June a new cargo began to be transported in the form of concrete housing parts manufactured by John Laing & Company. These were in the form of pre cast concrete sections of walls and floor units and were transported on the Manchester-London Freightliner.

The Saturday afternoon Ripple Lane-Southampton (Maritime) Freightliner passes St Denys on the final stage of its journey during June 1982. The containers with the 'Ford' branding on the wagons immediately behind Class 47 No.47339 were unusual to say the least. Regrettably both the signal box and the fine signal gantry visible in the background have since been swept away.

Michael J. Collins

This pair of Class 37s, Nos 37021 and 37074, have found a very heavy Coatbridge to Felixstowe train to take on the last part of its long journey to the Suffolk port on 6th August 1981. It will be no easy task to take such a well-loaded train down to Felixstowe even for two locomotives. Note the pair of Class 37s in the background which had brought the train down overnight throughout from Scotland. This area has since been completely modernised and this view is no longer possible because of overhead electric wiring.

Michael J. Collins

During the early 1980s Stratford Traction Depot gained a well-earned reputation for turning out very smart Class 47s complete with white roofs. On a crisp 30th December 1983 No.47311 approaches Manningtree station with a lightly loaded Freightliner from Willesden to Felixstowe.

Michael J. Collins

Road-rail competition on the GE main line. On 27th November 1983 a Garston-Felixstowe Freightliner behind Class 47 No.47014 shows a clean pair of heels to traffic on the parallel A12 dual carriageway at Springfield, north of Chelmsford.

Michael J. Collins

Class 37s Nos 37087 and 37010 will need all of their combined 3,500 hp to hoist the heavy 10.13 Stratford-Felixstowe North Freightliner train up Brentwood Bank. The pair were recorded about halfway up the bank on 25th August 1988.

Michael J. Collins

The Saturday 12.30 Birmingham Lawley Street-Southampton Maritime container train looked a bit short of business when it passed Aynho, south of Banbury, on 17th September 1988 with only six containers in the entire train. Traction was being provided by Class 47 No. 47008 on this occasion.

Michael J. Collins

Although the Felixstowe branch sees over twenty Freightliner movements midweek every 24-hours, operations are hampered because of line occupation problems on the single-track branch. Traversing the only passing loop on the branch at Derby Road are Class 37s Nos 37012 and 37087 with the 08.33 SO Stratford-Felixstowe South service. The leading locomotive saw several years service in Scotland and carried *Loch Rannoch* nameplates during this time.

Michael J. Collins

20

In June 1969 the Nottingham terminal was opened, with a second terminal in Birmingham sited near the city centre at Landor Street, opened in November. By late 1969 however, the bulk of the system was complete and over 140 Freightliner services were running every 24 hours. The network then consisted of 23 terminals with another ten privately owned terminals served by Freightliner. Since that time there have been a few additions and deletions from the network and services offered to customers but the die was cast and the system was up and running.

Table 2 details all of the regular Freightliner services operating in the 1989/90 timetable. It serves to give an up to date snapshot of the present ever changing system.

Table 2

Freightliner Services Timetable May 1989

Barking (Ripple Lane)

Depart	To	Arrive
05.50 EWD	TILBURY	06.32EWD
08.537SO	SOUTHAMPTON MCT	12.35SO
09.36SX	SOUTHAMPTON MCT	13.16SX
15.06SO	SOUTHAMPTON MCT	19.25SO
20.28SX	SOUTHAMPTON MCT	00.04MX

Barton Dock Road (Manchester)

Depart	To	Arrive
12.00SO	TILBURY	20.09SO
13.37SO	SOUTHAMPTON MCT	22.15SO
19.00SX	TILBURY	08.39SO
		09.03MSX
19.35SX	SOUTHAMPTON MCT	03.25MX

Birmingham (Lawley Street)

Depart	To	Arrive
03.48MX	SOUTHAMPTON MCT	08.05SO
		08.15MSX
	SOUTHAMPTON MILLBROOK	08.48SO
		08.55MSX
12.20SO	SOUTHAMPTON MCT	08.48SO
	TILBURY	20.09SO
15.03SX	HOLYHEAD	20.13SX
19.40SX	FELIXSTOWE NORTH	02.34MX
20.30SX	WILLESDEN	23.29SX
	TILBURY	06.06MX
20.45SX	COATBRIDGE	04.45MX
	HARWICH PQ.	05.39

Bristol

Depart	To	Arrive
13.50SX	COATBRIDGE	07.00MSX
		08.11SO
07.40SX	STRATFORD	04.43MX
	Ipswich Griffin Wharf	10.50SO
		12.50MSX
	Tilbury	09.37SO
		11.24MSX
	FELIXSTOWE SOUTH	11.52SO
		13.56MSX

Cardiff

Depart	To	Arrive
17.54SX	STRATFORD	23.31SX
	Southampton Millbrook	06.35MX
	Dagenham Storage	05.14MX
	IPSWICH GRIFFIN WHARF	10.50SO
	Tilbury	09.37SO
		11.24MSX
	FELIXSTOWE SOUTH	07.39MSX
		10.22SO

Depart	To	Arrive
18.30	COATBRIDGE	04.45MX
	HOLYHEAD	19.03MX

Cleveland

Depart	To	Arrive
13.51SX	LEEDS	17.12SX
	IMMINGHAM	13.43SX
	STRATFORD	02.38MX
	FELIXSTOWE SOUTH	11.52SO
		13.56MSX
17.30SX	SOUTHAMPTON MCT	01.28MX
	LEEDS	20.12MX
	FELIXSTOWE NORTH	03.02MX
	STRATFORD	02.38MX
	TILBURY	09.37SO
		11.24MSX
19.35SX	STRATFORD	02.06MX
	SOUTHAMPTON MILLBROOK	06.35MX
	HARWICH PARKESTON QUAY	09.43SO
		12.09MSX

Coatbridge

Depart	To	Arrive
00.05MX	GLASGOW	00.35MX
	WILLESDEN	09.08SO
	WILLESDEN	10.03MSX
	SOUTHAMPTON MILLBROOK	16.11MSX
	SOUTHAMPTON MCT	16.48MSX
07.10SO	SOUTHAMPTON MCT	18.37SO
15.00SX	BRISTOL	12.10SX
18.05SX	BIRMINGHAM	02.22MX
	CARDIFF	04.07MX
	STRATFORD	04.24MX
	SOUTHAMPTON MILLBROOK	06.10MX
19.03SX	GLASGOW	19.30SX
	GARSTON	05.19MX
	SEAFORTH	07.20MSX
		07.29SO
	WILLESDEN FSX	05.10MSX
	WILLESDEN FO	05.10SO
	SOUTHAMPTON MILLBROOK	11.01SO
19.40SX	STRATFORD	04.24MX
	Ipswich Griffin Wharf	10.50SO
		12.50MSX
	TILBURY	06.39MX
20.07SX	FELIXSTOWE NORTH	08.47MSX
		09.57SO
20.54SX	FELIXSTOWE NORTH	11.42SO
		12.03MSX

Dagenham Storage

Depart	To	Arrive
15.10SX	STRATFORD	15.32SX
19.20SX	STRATFORD	21.45SX

Felixstowe North

Depart	To	Arrive
03.50SX	STRATFORD	06.50MX
	BRISTOL	06.28MSX
		06.32SO
10.06SX	WILLESDEN	13.53SX
	GARSTON	03.08MX
	HOLYHEAD	10.03MX
	GLASGOW FSX	10.38MSX
	COATBRIDGE FO	10.38SO
18.27SX	LEEDS	00.31MX
	CLEVELAND	08.04MX
19.43SX	COATBRIDGE	07.48MX
21.54SX	TRAFFORD PARK	05.55MX
	GARSTON	06.57MX
22.45	TRAFFORD PARK	06.52MX
	HOLYHEAD	20.28SX

Felixstowe South

Depart	To	Arrive
06.23SX	LEEDS	19.17SX
	TRAFFORD PARK	23.12SX
10.08SX	GARSTON	19.47SX
16.48SX	COATBRIDGE	07.48MX
	STRATFORD	19.40MX
	Dagenham Storage	05.14MX
	Southampton Millbrook	06.35MX
	CARDIFF	06.31MX
	BRISTOL	06.28MX
		06.32SO
19.28SO	GARSTON	10.21MO
20.38SX	BIRMINGHAM	05.01MX

Garston

Depart	To	Arrive
05.37MX	SEAFORTH	07.20MSX
		10.23SO
07.32SX	FELIXSTOWE SOUTH	16.25SX
08.16SO	FELIXSTOWE SOUTH	16.43SO
		16.43SO
17.47SX	HOLYHEAD	23.13SX
	WILLESDEN	00.15MX
	STRATFORD	03.33MX
	Dagenham Storage	05.14MX
	Ipswich Griffin Wharf	10.50SO
		12.50MSX
	FELIXSTOWE SOUTH	11.52SO
		13.56MSX
	TILBURY	08.39SO
		09.03MSX
19.28SX	GLASGOW	02.00MX
	SOUTHAMPTON MILLBROOK	06.10MX
	SOUTHAMPTON MCT	06.35MX
21.53SX	HARWICH PARKESTON QUAY	05.39MX
	TILBURY	08.39SO
		09.03MSX

Seaforth

Depart	To	Arrive
18.15SX	As Required eg.	
	Harwich Parkeston Quay	05.39MX
	Tilbury	08.39MX
		09.03MSX
	Glasgow	02.00MX
	Willesden	00.15MX
	Stratford	03.33MX

Glasgow

Depart	To	Arrive
01.30MX	WILLESDEN	09.03SO
		10.03MSX
	SOUTHAMPTON MILLBROOK	16.11MSX
06.50SO	TRAFFORD PARK	13.11SO
	GARSTON	10.29MO
18.45SX	COATBRIDGE	19.08SX
	IPSWICH GRIFFIN WHARF	10.50SO
		12.50MSX
21.20SX	WILLESDEN	05.10MX
	SOUTHAMPTON MILLBROOK FO	11.01SO
	HARWICH PARKESTON QUAY	12.14SO
		14.27MSX
22.40SX	TRAFFORD PARK FSX	04.57MSX
	GARSTON	05.19MSX
	SEAFORTH	07.20MSX
		07.29SO

Holyhead

Depart	To	Arrive
04.00SO		09.29SO
05.38MSX	BIRMINGHAM	10.39MSX
06.13SX	TRAFFORD PARK FSX	11.11SX

Depart	To	Arrive
	SEAFORTH FO	12.08FO
	GARSTON	23.23SX
06.30MSX	WILLESDEN	13.12MSX
	STRATFORD	16.06MSX
17.56SX	HARWICH PARKESTON QUAY	05.39MX
	FELIXSTOWE SOUTH	16.25MSX
		16.43SO
	CARDIFF	04.07MX
23.01SUO	BIRMINGHAM	06.20MO
	WILLESDEN	06.10MO
	STRATFORD	07.17MO

Ipswich Griffin Wharf

Depart	To	Arrive
11.30SX	WILLESDEN	15.53SX
	BIRMINGHAM	03.27MX
17.00SX	STRATFORD	19.40SX

Immingham

Depart	To	Arrive
15.00SX	LEEDS	17.40SX
	CLEVELAND	13.16SX

Leeds

Depart	To	Arrive
02.17MX	STRATFORD	07.22MSX
	Ipswich Griffin Wharf	07.29SO
	TILBURY	09.37SO
		11.24MSX
05.11SX	CLEVELAND	08.04MX
10.22SX	CLEVELAND	13.16SX
11.03SO	TILBURY	20.09SO
11.19SX	IMMINGHAM	13.43SX
15.34SO	SOUTHAMPTON MCT	23.14SO
18.33SX	SOUTHAMPTON MCT	01.28MSX
21.10SX	FELIXSTOWE NORTH	03.02MX
21.50SX	STRATFORD	02.38MX
	Southampton Millbrook	06.35MX
	Dagenham Storage	05.14MX
	Ipswich Griffin Wharf FO	10.50SO
	FELIXSTOWE SOUTH	11.52SO
		13.56MSX

Harwich Parkeston Quay

Depart	To	Arrive
10.25SX	TRAFFORD PARK	20.52SX
	HOLYHEAD	23.13SX
17.19SX	STRATFORD	19.25SX
	Bristol	06.28MSX/
		06.32SO
	Cardiff	06.31MX
	Southampton Millbrook	06.35MX
	GARSTON	03.30MX
	LEEDS	04.27MX
	TRAFFORD PARK	07.15MX
20.02SX	WILLESDEN	01.04MX
	Glasgow FSX	10.38MSX
	Coatbridge FO	10.38SO
	BIRMINGHAM	05.01MX
	TRAFFORD PARK	06.52MX

Southampton MCT

Depart	To	Arrive
00.45MO	BARTON DOCK ROAD	07.49MO
02.40EWD	LEEDS	09.30SX/
		09.16SO
	Cleveland	13.16SX
05.10SO	BARKING	08.43SO
08.00SX	BARKING	11.23SX
12.50FO	COATBRIDGE	23.41FO
13.03SO	BIRMINGHAM	17.46SO
13.42FSX	COATBRIDGE	03.10MSX
15.51SX	BIRMINGHAM	21.24SX
19.43SX	BARKING	23.23SX
20.52SX	GARSTON	05.19MX

Depart	To	Arrive
23.04SUO	BARKING	02.15MO
23.47SX	BARTON DOCK ROAD	07.12MX

Southampton Millbrook

Depart	To	Arrive
14.52SX	WILLESDEN	17.40MX
	COATBRIDGE	03.10MX
18.06SX	STRATFORD	21.32SX
	Leeds	04.27MX
	Cleveland	08.04MX
	Dagenham Storage	05.14MX
	Ipswich Griffin Wharf	10.50SO
	Felixstowe South	07.39MSX
		10.22SO
20.04SX	TRAFFORD PARK	04.57MX
	GARSTON	05.19MX
	Seaforth	07.20MSX
		10.23SO

Stratford

Depart	To	Arrive
01.00MX	LEEDS	06.16MX
01.55MX	CARDIFF	06.31MX
	BRISTOL	06.28MSX
		06.32SO
02.19MX	TRAFFORD PARK	07.15MX
03.40MX	SOUTHAMPTON MILLBROOK	06.35MX
04.15MX	DAGENHAM STORAGE	05.14MX
04.28MX	IPSWICH GRIFFIN WHARF	10.50SO
		12.50MSX
	FELIXSTOWE SOUTH	07.39MSX
		10.22SO
07.54SO	HARWICH PARKESTON QUAY	09.53SO
10.20MSX		12.09MSX
08.33SO	FELIXSTOWE SOUTH	11.52SO
10.09MSX		13.56MSX
08.44SO	TILBURY	09.37SO
10.37MSX		11.24MSX
14.20SX	WILLESDEN	14.54SX
	HOLYHEAD	23.13SX
	COATBRIDGE	03.10MX
19.53SX	COATBRIDGE	05.05MX
21.00SX	CARDIFF	06.31MX
23.39SX	LEEDS	04.27MX
	CLEVELAND	08.04MX

Swindon

Depart	To	Arrive
02.45MX	STRATFORD	04.43MX
	TILBURY	06.39MX

Tilbury

Depart	To	Arrive
13.58SX	GARSTON	23.23SX
	TRAFFORD PARK	20.52SX
	BARTON DOCK ROAD	06.30MX
18.30SX	STRATFORD	19.09SX
	GARSTON	03.30MX
	COATBRIDGE	05.05MX
19.55SX	WILLESDEN	21.47SX
	BIRMINGHAM	03.27MX
20.47SX	STRATFORD	21.45SX

Depart	To	Arrive
	SWINDON	01.29SX
21.00SUO	BIRMINGHAM	06.20MO
	LEEDS	06.32MO
	BARTON DOCK ROAD	07.15MO
21.30SX	BARKING	22.19SX
21.35SUO		22.25SUO
21.47SX	LEEDS	06.16MX
	FELIXSTOWE SOUTH	11.52SO
		13.56MSX

Trafford Park

Depart	To	Arrive
01.20MX	TILBURY	8.39SO
		09.03MSX
	WILLESDEN MSX	13.12MSX
	FELIXSTOWE SOUTH	16.25MSX
		16.43SO
03.00MX	CLEVELAND	08.57MX
15.37SX	HOLYHEAD	20.28SX
16.07FO	GLASGOW	01.49SO
19.55SX	GLASGOW	02.00MX
	PARKESTON QUAY	05.39MX
21.53SX	WILLESDEN	01.49MX
	STRATFORD	03.33MX
22.34SX	FELIXSTOWE NORTH	05.37MX

Willesden

Depart	To	Arrive
00.20MX	BIRMINGHAM	03.27MX
02.04MSX	GLASGOW	10.38MSX
02.04SO	COATBRIDGE	10.38SO
03.00MX	STRATFORD	03.33MX
03.40MX	TRAFFORD PARK	07.15MX
04.40MX	TILBURY	06.06MX
07.45SO	FELIXSTOWE SOUTH	11.52SO
	HARWICH PARKESTON QUAY	12.14SO
08.10SO	SOUTHAMPTON MILLBROOK	11.01SO
10.06MSX	FELIXSTOWE SOUTH	13.56MSX
	HARWICH PARKESTON QUAY	14.27MSX
13.50MSX	SOUTHAMPTON MILLBROOK	16.11MSX
	SOUTHAMPTON MCT	16.48MSX
16.25SX	HOLYHEAD	23.13SX
19.10SX	COATBRIDGE	03.10MX
21.15SX	COATBRIDGE	05.05MX
21.50	GARSTON	03.08MX
	HOLYHEAD	10.03MX
	TRAFFORD PARK	04.57MX

Notes:
In this table the following format has been used:
UPPER CASE = Direct Train Services
Lower Case = Link Services

Abbreviations:

SX	=	Monday to Friday inclusive
FSX	=	Monday to Thursday inclusive
MX	=	Tuesday to Saturday inclusive
MSX	=	Tuesday to Friday inclusive
FO	=	Friday only
SO	=	Saturday only
SUO	=	Sunday only
EWD	=	Each Weekday

Inclement Weather

On 29th March 1984 Class 47 No.47212 approaches Reddish Traction Depot with the 15.54 Trafford Park to Holyhead service. In heavy rain the train had slipped almost to a stand at this point.

Steve Turner

Clinging fine rain was blowing in from the North Sea on 29th December 1989 as Class 37s Nos 37053 and 37426 *Y Lein Fach/Vale of Rheidol* struggled for adhesion as they joined the single track Felixstowe branch after traversing the hill from North Terminal with the 10.06 service to Stratford. The Class 37/4 was a rare bird in these parts but had recently been transferred to Immingham and made a brief appearance in East Anglia during this period, hence the photograph at Trimley.

Michael J. Collins

In a heavy autumnal drizzle Class 47 No. 47286 approaches Junction Road Junction, on the North London Line with a Ripple Lane-Southampton working on 25th September 1986.

Michael J. Collins

One of the strengths of the Freightliner system is that merchandise stands a good chance of getting through on time even in the most dire conditions. On a foggy day like 27th November 1982 the motorways would have been very hard going. Class 47 No. 47142 heads the 09.36 Ripple Lane-Southampton (Maritime) working through a fog-bound West Ealing station. If the station clock is reliable the train is a few minutes early!

Michael J. Collins

Early morning fog is just beginning to clear as Class 47 No.47451 gingerly eases its way through Acton South Junction with the 08.10 SO Willesden-Southampton (Millbrook) service. By this time a number of Class 47s equipped with electric train heat were becoming surplus to requirements in the passenger sectors and it was not uncommon to see one on a Freightliner train.

Michael J. Collins

Penetrating the snow covered tracks at Colwyn Bay with a Holyhead bound Freightliner is Class 40 No.40172 on 11th December 1981. Travel by road in such conditions would be hazardous but the trains usually manage to get through.
Larry Goddard

Behind Class 31 No.31112 are hidden the 'up' and 'down' slow lines to the Erewash Valley route at Clay Cross Junction. These had not been ploughed because of a dispute as to which sector should pay for the exercise – Railfreight or Provincial Services? The tracks were still covered in drifts up to six feet deep as the Saturday Leeds-Rugby (for Tilbury on Monday) Freightliner passes by. It is a debacle such as this which puts in jeopardy the competitive edge which rail has over road in conditions such as these.
Dr L. A. Nixon

With the snows of winter proving reluctant to disappear the 11.35 Stratford-Felixstowe Freightliner passes Hatfield Peverel on 10th January 1985 behind Class 47 No.47115.
Michael J. Collins

Chapter 4

Rail Traction

Class 47s

One of the first locomotives ever to haul a Freightliner train was Class 40 No.D371 which, on 5th May 1965, hauled a test train of prototype wagons northwards from Crewe with the dynamometer car coupled next to the locomotive. Testing continued for some months but the first commercial Freightliner on 15th November 1965 was hauled on the initial stage of its journey from Maiden Lane depot to the WCML by a Class 47. This was highly appropriate because, although in theory any locomotive fitted with air brakes can operate a Freightliner train, there can be no doubt that Class 47s have operated more Freightliner trains than any other diesel locomotive type. Their wide route availability (they can go almost everywhere on the BR system) combined with good haulage capability, makes them ideal machines for providing traction for Freightliners. Another advantage is that they are almost universally known by train crews throughout the BR network. They can thus be diagrammed for a train which traverses several regions, with little fear that rostered train crews at key stages along the route will not be able to take over the train for want of traction knowledge. The Southern Region, for example, only briefly had an allocation of Class 47s of its own when some

In 'Constable Country' the 16.48 SX Felixstowe-Stratford service is powered up Dedham Bank by Class 47 No.47539 *Rochdale Pioneers* on 14th June 1988. This locomotive is now dedicated to haulage of parcels trains and is unlikely to appear on Freightliner trains with any regularity again.

Michael J. Collins

In the author's opinion the Class 47s have never looked better than when in the original two-tone green livery which suited them so well. In this condition No.D1762 approaches Purfleet Rifle Range crossing with a Willesden-Tilbury service on 2nd March 1973. This locomotive was later named *County of Essex* in a ceremony held at Witham station in July 1979.

Brian Morrison

were diagrammed for Waterloo-Bournemouth services pending electrification. A large number of crews are passed for driving them, however, and they have been seen on Southern metals heading Freightliner trains for over twenty years. An early appearance of a Class 47 on such a working occurred on 29th January 1968 when No. D1101 (47518) was seen passing Farnborough heading towards Southampton with a Freightliner train that was being run in conjunction with the opening of Millbrook Terminal later that day. The first train to arrive at Southampton Maritime Terminal was powered by Class 47 No.1820 (47339) on 2nd April 1972. On 15th February 1986 Class 47/4 No.47457 was named *Ben Line* in a ceremony held at Southampton station in recognition of that company's contribution to Freightliner traffic over several years.

It was on 22nd April 1968 that a real milestone in Class 47 haulage of Freightliner trains occurred when No. D1758 (47164) was adorned with a Union Jack and a Tricolour flag when it hauled the very first London-Paris Freightliner away from Stratford depot.

Other Type 4s and 5s

It has already been remarked that a Class 40 was an early performer on a test Freightliner train in 1965 and they were used on a number of test workings in those early days before Freightliners commenced revenue earning operations. In the fullness of time these ponderous locomotives became associated with the haulage of Freightliner trains in certain parts of the country before they were withdrawn in the late 1970s and early 1980s. Class 40s were particularly common on workings in the Manchester and Liver-

Class 40s hauled thousands of Freightliner trains in their twenty year life but this example has strayed well off the beaten track. Recorded passing Northam Junction, Southampton, was No.40012 (*Aureol*) on a Freightliner train bound for Coatbridge on a spring-like 12th April 1984.
Mrs Jean Marsden

The 12.15 Lawley Street (Birmingham)-Nottingham service passes North Staffordshire Junction near Burton-on-Trent on 25th October 1983. This service often produced a Class 45 at this time and on this day it duly obliged with No. 45036.

Michael J. Collins

Although about half the Class 52 'Westerns' were, in time, fitted with air-braking equipment it was most unusual to see one hauling a Freightliner train. This is because most liner workings are inter-regional and comparatively few drivers outside the Western Region had the necessary traction knowledge to handle them. Nevertheless No. D1009 *Western Invader* was captured on film passing Ruscombe, near Twyford, on 9th March 1976 with a 'down' train for South Wales.

John A. M. Vaughan

Class 50 No.D406 (since withdrawn) descends Beattock with a well loaded 'up' service from Glasgow in 1968. This was during the period when the class were allocated to Crewe Diesel Depot for service on WCML trains over the northern fells, prior to electrification. The Class 50s were not uncommon on such trains at this time.

When the Class 50s were transferred to the Western Region following completion of the electrification of the WCML, appearances on Freightliner trains became much less frequent. One service which did occasionally turn up a class member was the 12.15 Lawley Street FLT-Nottingham FLT train and the return balancing working. This was the case on 4th July 1986 when Class 50 No.50027 *Lion* was the only available power for the diagram. It is seen here passing the site of the former Branston station south of Burton-on-Trent in charge of the 15.35 Nottingham FLT-Lawley Street FLT service.

John Tuffs

Class 44 type ever appearing on a Freightliner but members of all sub-classes of Class 45 and 46 worked regularly. They performed frequently out of Nottingham Terminal on services to Birmingham but one of their notable stamping grounds was on the long haul trains between Newcastle (Follingsby) Terminal and Cardiff or Danycraig (Swansea). These Freightliners would be worked throughout via the North East-South West route arriving in Wales via Gloucester and Chepstow. Following withdrawal of the Class 40s the Class 45s also worked regularly on the North Wales coast line to Holyhead for a couple of years until their own ultimate withdrawal from service. An early appearance of a 'Peak' in East Anglia – indeed the very first appearance of a Class 46 in this part of the country – occurred on 16th April 1969 when No.148 (46011) worked into Ipswich with a Freightliner service for Harwich returning light engine to March.

A number of the hydraulic 'Western' Class 52s were fitted with air brakes late in life to enable them to haul Mark II passenger stock and, in theory, they could thus haul Freightliner trains. In practice they were rare birds indeed on such trains but sometimes a failure of the rostered locomotive would press them in to emergency service. One such occasion was recorded on 5th September 1968 when the Par-Park Royal Freightliner was handled by No.D1051 *Western Ambassador*. Also in the consist was a vacuum head of ten ordinary covered wagons together with a brake van at the rear. Since the Class 52 was not fitted with any train air braking at this time it must be assumed that the vacuum wagons were placed in the train to assist with braking.

Class 50s were common on Freightliner workings during the 1960s and 1970s when they were all based at Crewe. They would often work very heavy Freightliners northwards from Crewe to Glasgow, sometimes working over Shap but more often in the later part of the period via Preston, Blackburn, Hellifield and the Settle and Carlisle line. They took the latter route when line occupation was at a premium due to electrification work on the northern fells or to prevent line occupation problems for following expresses which were often delayed anyway because of electrification work. BR liked to give their Anglo-Scottish expresses priority at this time because they were suffering from competition with the airlines. Completion of the WCML electrification saw all the Class 50s transferred en block to the Western Region. In the years immediately following their transfer the Class 50s became rare traction indeed for

A very rare photograph indeed. Class 55 'Deltic' No.D9004 *Queen's Own Highlander* crosses Welwyn Viaduct with the 18.55 King's Cross-Aberdeen Freightliner on 4th August 1969. Appearances of 'Deltics' on liner trains can be counted on the fingers of one hand.
David Percival

pool area to Holyhead via Chester and the North Wales Coast Line but they also put in a large number of appearances on the ECML, certainly north of Doncaster. In Scotland too, they were common on Freightliner trains from Portobello Terminal, Edinburgh and on workings to and from Aberdeen Terminal.

Although originally considered to be passenger locomotives, the Sulzer engined cousins of the Class 40s – the 'Peaks'– became, in time, common traction for Freightliner trains. No reference has been found of a member of the

Class 56s made more frequent appearances on Freightliner trains in the early 1980s than they do today because sectorisation of locomotive fleets has decreed that they stick mainly to coal and aggregates haulage. On 23rd July 1983 the driver of Class 56 No.56071 climbs down from his mount to enquire the reason for being halted at signals at Leamington Spa while in charge of a Lawley Street-Southampton working. The Class 56 is likely to have been changed for a Class 47 at Oxford or Reading.
Michael J. Collins

During the national coal miners' strike Class 56s were used on some Freightliner trains instead of coal trains to keep them in good condition while they were being under-utilised. On 21st April 1984 No.56074 *Kellingly Colliery* was recorded passing Bescot station with an 'up' train. Note the orange flashing light mounted above the cab which this machine carried experimentally for some years. It was used to warn lineside staff of the locomotive's silent approach when working in power stations.

John A. M. Vaughan

The photographer was fortunate to record the unique Class 56, No.56042, which is mounted on CP1 bogies, as it came off the Aston line at Stechford, Birmingham, with the 12.30 Lawley Street-Southampton Freightliner on 13th March 1982.

Geoff Dowling

Making a rare appearance on a Freightliner train is Railfreight Construction sub-sector Class 37 No.37043 working in multiple with No.37128. The train is the 04.28 Stratford-Felixstowe North service and the duo were recorded on the Felixstowe branch just south of Derby Road on 26th March 1988. No.37043 spent a considerable time in the Highlands and carried *Loch Lomond* nameplates for some years.

Michael J. Collins

A short ten-wagon set such as this is well within the capabilities of a single Class 31. Passing Rainham Marshes on the LTS is No.5599 hauling a Barking-Tilbury Freightliner portion which had been detached from a longer train at Ripple Lane sidings, 23rd August 1973.
John Rickard

Running as a special is this Leeds-Tilbury Freightliner recorded heading up the ECML at Hitchin on a Saturday afternoon in August 1981. Traction was being provided by Class 31 No.31130.

Michael J. Collins

haulage of Freightliner trains because their work was confined almost entirely to express passenger work. By the 1980s, however, much of this work was taken over by High Speed Trains and Class 50s began to appear occasionally on Freightliners again. Typical workings were the 18.09 Bristol-Swindon (Cocklebury)-Stratford Freightliner which they would work as far as Swindon and also a number of workings in the Midlands would occasionally produced a Class 50 when one was being worked south following works attention at Doncaster. In 1983 the Birmingham Lawley Street-Ipswich OCL 'Company' Freightliner was booked a Class 50 as far as Nuneaton. To the disappointment of local enthusiasts, more often than not it produced a Class 47 but on 17th February 1983 No.50026 *Indomitable* arrived at the Warwickshire town followed by No.50014 *Warspite* two nights later. Class 50s have appeared on this turn fairly regularly thereafter.

Appearances by Class 55 'Deltics' on Freightliner workings were extremely rare but a couple of occasions when this happened have been recorded. On 14th June 1968 No.D9020 (55020) *Nimbus* hauled a Freightliner from Edinburgh Portobello Terminal to King's Cross and the 18.55 King's Cross-Aberdeen Freightliner was hauled by No.D9004 (55004) *Queen's Own Highlander* on 4th August 1969. Of slightly higher power than the 'Deltics' was the Brush 4,000 hp prototype No.HS4000 *Kestrel*. This had protracted trials on BR and for some months in 1970 its regular working was the overnight Hull-Stratford Freightliner and balancing return working. Unfortunately most of this work was done during the hours of darkness and no photograph has been traced.

The BR purpose-built freight locomotives of Class 56 were introduced between 1976 and 1984. They are used mostly on bulk hauls of coal and stone but they have appeared regularly on Freightliner trains over the years. These occurrences are seen most frequently in the East Midlands area and in the Birmingham area but they have appeared as far south as Southampton on these workings from time to time. On 2nd February 1990 Class 56 No. 56078 arrived at Ipswich shortly after 17.00 in connection with a crew training exercise which was taking place locally. The motive power situation was so dire that it was

immediately pressed into service – the traction inspector who was to do the training volunteered to drive. It worked the Ipswich to Felixstowe leg of a Garston to Felixstowe South Freightliner and then worked light engine over to North Terminal. Here it provided traction as far as Ipswich on the overnight Freightliner to Coatbridge. It became the first Class 56 ever to work on the Felixstowe branch but, of course, they are well known in the Ipswich area on stone trains, albeit with March crews although in early 1990 Ipswich crews were themselves trained on Class 56s.

The Class 58 heavy freight locomotives were built between 1983 and 1987. Again, this type of locomotive is used mainly on bulk coal hauls but appearances of the type on Freightliner trains have occurred several times over the years. During 1984 and 1985 a train running on Saturdays Only from Birmingham Lawley Street to Southampton was booked for Class 58 haulage as far as Banbury or Oxford via Coventry. Unfortunately, only once did the Class 58 get all the way down to the South Coast due to a replacement locomotive not being available on the Western Region. Another Freightliner service booked a Class 58 on a semi-regular basis was the Lawley Street-Nottingham service and 15.21 return. The formation of this train was usually just one five-set of wagons and was well within the haulage

The 11.05 SO Leeds-Bescot 'up' loop Freightliner approaches the town of Water Orton on 5th March 1983. Although well loaded Class 31 No.31118 would easily handle this short train.

Bert Wynn

capability of a Class 58. Regrettably the service ceased to run from April 1987 when Nottingham Terminal closed. The class have also been turned out on the evening Lawley Street to Felixstowe working which they take as far as Nuneaton where the train hands over to electric haulage.

The Smaller Diesels

Other, less powerful diesel types have hauled Freightliner trains over the last 25 years or so but their areas of operation have been more localised. In the early days of Freightliner, personnel in each geographical area had to be trained in their safe operation. One of the first instances of a Class 37 hauling a Freightliner train in East Anglia occurred on 22nd July 1968 when driver training began between Bury St Edmunds, Whitemoor and Lincoln. Running under headcode 3G66 and signalled by the usual liner train bell code of 3-2-5, the train, headed by No.D6962 (37262), left Whitemoor at 10.30. Consisting of an unusual formation of just three wagons it proceeded to Bury St Edmunds via Ely and Soham where it was booked to arrive at 12.00. Here

the locomotive ran round its train and left at 12.45 for Whitemoor and onwards to Lincoln Holmes Yard. The train then ran back to Whitemoor where it was stabled at the steam engine running shed at March. This pattern continued for some months until all train crews knew the techniques for handling Freightliner trains. To this day, Class 37s are strongly associated with liner trains in East Anglia, working in pairs from Stratford to Felixstowe.

A flashback to the late 1960s when Gateshead had an allocation of Class 25s. At Pelaw, Tyne and Wear, Class 25 No.D7593 passes with an empty Freightliner set for Follingsby Terminal while a Middlesbrough-Newcastle dmu scuttles past on the right.

Ian S. Carr

During 1985 a Saturdays Only Holyhead-Southampton Freightliner was introduced. From Birmingham this working utilised the Class 33 which had been stabled overnight at Saltley after working the previous evening's Fridays Only Portsmouth-Leeds passenger train as far as the West Midlands. On 3rd September 1983 it was Class 33/1 No.33101 that was photographed heading south at Appleford, near Didcot, making for the Southern Region.
Michael J. Collins

The Holyhead-Southampton Freightliner again but this time on the Southern as it passes Bramley, between Reading and Basingstoke. Traction on this occasion was supplied by Class 33/0 No.33051.
Michael J. Collins

In recent years, since electrification of the GE main line and the North London freight link, their work has been poached somewhat by electric types working through from the WCML. A fleet of Class 37s will be required in the foreseeable future, however, based at Ipswich for powering Freightliner trains along the non-electrified branch from Ipswich to Felixstowe. The Freightliner trains from East Anglia to other parts of the country have also become associated with Class 37 haulage. For several years there has been two Freightliner trains diagrammed to run nightly from Felixstowe to Glasgow (Coatbridge). Usually at least one of these trains is operated by a pair of Class 37s which operate the train throughout to Scotland via Peterborough and the ECML. The same pair of locomotives are usually booked to haul the southbound train the next evening after having accomplished at least one round trip on an ore train between Hunterston and Ravenscraig as a fill in turn. In recognition of the long association of Class 37 with Freightliner trains, No.37358 was named *P & O Containers* in a ceremony held at Southampton on 13th April 1988.

A rare picture indeed of unusual traction for the 13.14 Trafford Park-Tilbury Freightliner on 16th January 1988. Manchester Ship Canal 0-6-0 diesel shunter No.4002 (Hudswell Clarke D1076 of 1959) is seen under the 25kV ac catenary at Trafford Park Terminal. Few privately owned diesels ever haul Freightliner trains on BR property although at Felixstowe South former BR Class 10 shunter No.D3489 *Colonel Tomline* is used to shunt Freightliners on the premises of the Felixstowe Dock & Harbour Board.

Dr L. A. Nixon

Although more numerous, the Class 31s are less common as hauliers of liner trains. They do sometimes appear however, more often deputising for one failed Class 37 out of a pair. This then provides the novel sight of a pair of disparate locomotives powering a Freightliner train. In East Anglia, pairs of Class 31s are also known on liner trains – again working in lieu of a pair of Class 37s – but they are not regarded as sufficiently powerful to haul a heavy train on their own. They have occasionally been seen single handed on five or ten-set trains.

The Southern Region Class 33 "Cromptons" have had a number of turns on Freightliner trains over the years. In the 1970s they used to work right through to the West Midlands on the Southampton to Dudley services returning the same day with the balancing working. During the late 1970s and early 1980s they regularly worked in pairs from Willesden Terminal right through to Southampton. In the mid-1980s Class 33s could be seen on wide ranging passenger turns which took them as far as West Wales and Holyhead on long cyclic diagrams from Eastleigh depot. At this time they were known by large numbers of BR train crews on both the London Midland and Western regions in addition to their home region. It was inevitable that they turned up on Freightliner trains in parts of the country well away from their native Southern Region. They had a number of turns on the Birmingham to Oxford via Banbury line in the mid-1980s.

On 27th August 1988 the totally unexpected happened when a pair of "Cromptons" worked right through to East Anglia on a Freightliner. The Southampton area was obviously short of power when Nos 33035 and 33209 were put on an extra Southampton Maritime to Felixstowe service which they proceeded to work through to Ipswich. The pair caused quite a stir when they roared through Ipswich station. At the time of writing the end is near for the Class 33s because classified repairs on the type have been stopped. Their Freightliner workings on the Southern have been taken over by more powerful locomotives and their sphere of work is now almost completely tied to that region. It looks as if few more appearances on Freightliners will be recorded.

The Class 25s, although not particularly powerful, were known to be tenacious little machines particularly when operated in pairs. They were quite frequently to be seen on Freightliner trains in the West Midlands area and would often get down to the south end of the WCML as far as Willesden in lieu of an electric locomotive. They were also frequently seen on the Midland line heading liner trains out of Nottingham Terminal and sometimes operated single-handed on those occasions when the daily train to Lawley Street was lightly loaded. The "Fletliner" brick trains between both Stewartby and Garston and Stewartby and King's Cross were the preserve almost exclusively of pairs of Class 25s. Their Scottish cousins, the Class 26s have always been very rare on liner trains but one report has been found documenting when No. D5302 (26002) worked a southbound train of empty Freightliner flats from Edinburgh Terminal up to Newcastle.

Class 76 1,500V dc electrics were common sights on Freightliner trains over the Woodhead route across the Pennines before it closed in July 1981. With only a month to go before final closure Class 76s Nos 76021 and 76026 pass Torside heading from Yorkshire into Lancashire on 16th June 1981.

Paul D. Shannon

Electric Traction

Surprisingly it was not on the West Coast Main Line that Freightliner trains were first seen being hauled by electric traction. This honour fell to the Woodhead Route between Manchester and Sheffield which was electrified using the 1,500 dc overhead system. A number of liner trains were booked to operate over this route and, although diesel substitutions sometimes occurred, they were usually operated by pairs of the Class 76 electrics which were associated with the route. These electrics were extremely capable machines and a pair could easily handle a fully loaded 20-set on this steeply graded main line. Regrettably, after much protest from both the public and staff alike the line

Passing Hanslope high speed junction the 06.30 MSX Holyhead-Willesden Freightliner heads south on the WCML behind Class 85 No.85015. The first generation of 25kV ac electrics have hauled vast numbers of Freightliners on this route over the years. The photograph is dated 27th July 1988.

Michael J. Collins

An early shot of Class 86 No.E3148 in original 'electric blue' livery passing Willesden northbound with a uniform rake of Freightliners' own containers. This locomotive has since been renumbered 86432 and subsequently 86632. It is allocated to the Railfreight sector and thus still does a large amount of container train haulage today.

Colin J. Marsden

One of the Class 86/3s which were fitted with multiple working equipment so that they could be used in pairs on heavy freights traversing the northern fells. This time working single-handed, on the south end of the WCML where gradients are not quite so taxing, is Class 86/3 No.86313. It is seen on the 'up' slow line hauling a Halewood-Felixstowe 'company' train of Ford Motor Co. containers past Castlethorpe, Northamptonshire, on 27th October 1981. This locomotive has since been renumbered 86413.

Michael J. Collins

Class 86/4 No. 86426 was repainted into near-original livery and carried its original number E3195 during 1988. The locomotive draws into Bescot alongside the M6 with a Coatbridge-Southampton Freightliner on 28th January 1989.

John Whitehouse

Through working of 25kV ac locomotives from the WCML to the Anglia Region was possible following electrification of the North London Line. On 15th May 1989, the first day of such working, Nos 86438 and 86401 *Northampton Town* pass Marks Tey, south of Colchester with the 16.48 Harwich Parkeston Quay to Garston service.

Michael J. Collins

closed from 20th July 1981 and liner trains were forced to cross the Pennines diesel powered by another route.

The mainstay of electric haulage of Freightliner trains in recent years has been on the West Coast route where large numbers of liner trains are operated by 25kV ac electrics over the whole route between London and Scotland. The full range of electrics from Class 81 to Class 87 have been noted in command of liner trains on this route since electrification. Loadings on the route tend to be heavy but south of Crewe a single locomotive can usually cope with all but the most taxing of trains. The heavy grades over the northern fells such as Shap and Beattock are a different proposition however, and here most Freightliner trains are rostered for haulage by a pair of electrics. Only certain locomotives (of Classes 86/4 and 87) are equipped with the necessary multiple working equipment to allow this to take place. Despite this, only ten years ago an electric locomotive could be noted powering a West Coast route Freightliner northwards in the morning and it was quite possible to see the same machine heading southwards with an express passenger later the same day. The impact of sectorisation of the railways in the late 1980s made this less possible. Now each traffic division has its own assets, including locomotives. Only locomotives owned by the Railfreight Distribution sub sector are permitted to handle Freightliner trains except in times of dire emergency. The Class 86/4s are now designated a Railfreight asset and thus haul Freightliner trains – as well as normal freight turns – but the Class 87s are now seldom seen on freight because they are regarded as InterCity assets.

The 25kV ac electrification of the North London lines allowed through running of electric locomotives on Freightliner trains from the WCML to East Anglia. Although electrification of the route was completed some months previously, through running did not begin on a regular basis until 15th May 1989. Within four months all existing representatives of Class 86/4 had visited East Anglia on these trains.

The latest ac electric at work on the West Coast route is the Class 90 which began to be delivered from Crewe Works in 1987. First deliveries were destined for the InterCity sector but Railfreight soon put in an order for these very powerful locomotives. Although fitted with multiple working equipment, Railfreight view them as machines with sufficient power to obviate the necessity of double-heading even the heaviest trains over Shap and Beattock.

Sectorisation of the locomotive fleet and other BR assets has decreed that at the time of writing all Class 87s belong to the InterCity sector. Appearances on Freightliner trains have become rare but when this photograph was taken such workings were commonplace. Class 87 No.87006 *City of Glasgow* partners Class 86/3 No.86313 past Crawford with a 'down' Freightliner on 16th April 1982.

Dr L. A. Nixon

Brand new on the Freightliner traction scene are the Class 90s introduced to traffic in 1987. By 1989 Railfreight Distribution had some on order and trials took place on Freightliner test trains on both the ECML and the GE main line. One of these trials is recorded passing Manningtree on 7th August 1989 with Class 90 No.90030 leading Test Car 10, Class 47 No.47234 and 25 Freightliner wagons ballasted with old rails. The ensemble worked through from Willesden to Ipswich Yard and return.

Michael J. Collins

At the time of writing the Railfreight members of this class had not entered service and discussions were taking place as to whether it would be a good idea to remove the electric train heat equipment from them so that they could not be appropriated by any other BR sector. Railfreight had managed to borrow an InterCity example however, and train crews on the both the West Coast route and in East Anglia were being trained in their operation.

Freightliner Locomotive Maintenance

Prior to 1987 locomotives were allocated a home depot.

Routine maintenance however, was often carried out at a location other than its home base. Major repairs were sometimes referred to selected depots in the area with the necessary facilities and equipment. Locomotives would be fairly wide ranging at this time in terms of types of trains handled and areas of the country covered. Furthermore, it would be common to see an individual locomotive handling a Freightliner train one day and then see it operating a passenger train the next day.

Sectorisation in 1987, changed all that. Since then each locomotive is dedicated to a particular sector and to a particular traffic flow. Only in the most dire of circumstances does a particular machine stray from its dedicated work. The diesel traction which operates Freightliner trains is now owned by the Railfreight Distribution sub sector. At first some of this sector's Class 37s were maintained at Stratford depot but more recently the entire Railfreight Distribution fleet has been maintained at Tinsley Depot, Sheffield. Similarly, all the electric locomotives working Freightliner trains on both the WCML and Anglia Region sponsored by Railfreight Distribution are now maintained at Crewe Electric Depot.

Diesels in Multiple

Class 47s are not fitted with multiple working equipment so it is uncommon to see two working together. Train paths on the single track Felixstowe branch are at a premium however, and sometimes it is necessary to double-head trains to get one locomotive back to Ipswich instead of working it back light engine. This was the case on 21st March 1987 when Nos 47287 and 47237 were photographed heading a Felixstowe-Stratford extra Freightliner at Levington. Both locomotives were under power at the time.

Michael J. Collins

A very unusual Class 20, No. 20146 plus Class 37, No. 37157 pairing was recorded at Port Glasgow on 15th April 1982. The train is a Freightliner to Clydeport near Greenock and the ensemble was hauling a train of OCL containers. The River Clyde is visible in the background.

Dr L. A. Nixon

Class 47 to the rescue! When hauling the heavy 07.10 SO Coatbridge-Southampton Freightliner Class 33 No.33040 had failed in the Birmingham area. This accounts for the strange pairing with Class 47 No. 47005 as the duo passed Birmingham International on 4th June 1988. The Class 33 was being given a tow onto home territory.

Steve Turner

Another strange pairing but this time both locomotives were under power. The 19.20 Lawley Street-Felixstowe Freightliner was booked for traction by a pair of locomotives as far as Nuneaton for a time during 1983. Class 47 No.47166 leads Class 25 No.25258 past Washwood Heath Sidings on 6th September 1983.

Geoff Dowling

Disparate liveried Class 37s Nos 37004 and 37055 head the 19.43 Felixstowe North Terminal-Coatbridge service along the Felixstowe branch near Orwell on 13th June 1988. This pair of locomotives will run round the train on arrival at Ipswich and power it right through to Scotland overnight.

Michael J. Collins

Catching a shaft of low winter sunlight are Class 58s Nos 58027 and 58036 as they take the main line south out of Lawley Street with the 12.25 service to Southampton Maritime on 27th December 1986.

John Whitehouse

Another Birmingham scene but this time at Bescot with triple headed Class 25s – all working! On 23rd June 1984 Nos 25205 + 25185 + 25187 head south with a Freightliner bound for Willesden. How far this ensemble worked the train is, unfortunately, not known.

Michael J. Collins

Class 31 plus Class 37 duos are not common but they do occasionally occur. This Felixstowe-Willesden Freightliner was originally booked for its usual two Class 37s but one of the pair had failed. Struggling with their heavy load up Belstead Bank, south of Ipswich, are Nos 31284 and 37032 in December 1985.

Michael J. Collins

Chapter 5

The Terminals

Cranes

The initial choice for cranes in the earliest terminals was the Drott Travelift. In all, fourteen were bought and they were of the portal crane type spanning both road and rail tracks. The type was developed over a ten year period in the United States and was equipped with a grappler frame whose legs enabled it to lift containers between 10 and 30 feet long by means of bottom lift pockets. The machines were diesel powered and hydraulically operated and were mounted on pneumatic tyres. They could thus be moved from one part to another of the terminal for maintenance – a major benefit lost when the later rail-mounted cranes were purchased.

By the late 1960s the limitations of the Travelift crane began to cause problems. It was just not designed for continuous working over twenty-four hours, day after day. Traffic had grown immensely and the cranes were being pushed beyond their limits. The solution was to buy some electric rail-mounted cranes from Herbert Morris of Leicester and a number of these are still in use today. They are again of the portal type and were of Class 3 specification. It was thought necessary for the cranes to be capable of handling train loads of 35 – 40 containers within two hours. Such speed of operation was absolutely necessary to ensure cost effective use of rail rolling stock and to cope with the daily peaks of road vehicles arriving at the terminals.

The next generation of cranes were even larger. They were massive by railway standards and larger than those commonly in use at major ports. Termed 'Goliath' cranes they were of cantilever construction and of 2-6-2 and 2-6-3 configuration. The first two were installed at Willesden Freightliner depot and were capable of passing the largest containers broadside between their legs and turning it through 330 degrees. This attribute meant that it was no longer necessary to turn trains en route in order to ensure correct positioning of container doors for traffic flow in the terminal. Another benefit found was that traffic vulnerable to pilfering or downright theft could easily be loaded with

container doors innermost to minimise such risks. The cranes were supplied with a guarantee of 3,000 hours annual utilisation at full load. The plan was for BR to work these cranes for 18 hours a day and the cranes had a capacity to handle an average of 25 containers per hour. The new cranes were capable of much enhanced performance compared with the hydraulic cranes which were used when the Freightliner service was in its infancy.

The new crane was designed to exploit its maximum utilisation potential. The cab was fitted out for comfort and efficiency of operation. A fully upholstered adjustable seat for the operator, opening windows sporting lightly tinted glass, heating and demisting equipment and wide-vision window wipers which operated in a straight line, were all features embodied in the cab design. Sighting marks, applied on the cab front window and on the Freightliner wagon frames, aided longitudinal positioning for engaging and positioning boxes and a sight mark on the crane bridge aided lateral positioning over the respective tracks. Another objective was ease and speed of maintenance together with quick repair in the event of an accident or failure. The early machines of this type had a rotary converter to provide dc crane power from industrial supplies but solid state equipment was fitted in later models. All wiring and electric circuits were preassembled and installed on a plug-in basis and spare components held in stock at strategic locations. The grappler frame is quickly replaceable and spare serviceable frames held in stock. The cranes, therefore, have been reliable mostly and have been refurbished at intervals to extend their lives. Recurrent electronic failures with the thyristor control on cranes of the Arrol design was the greatest shortcoming and this led to the adoption of a simpler form of control gear at Southampton Maritime Terminal. There have also been some mechanical failures over the years such as excessive gear bearing wear. In the late 1970s problems emerged with the concrete beams on which the cranes rest. Once again, this problem was caused by increased traffic and the sheer intensity of working. Subsidence, causing cracking between piles and rail fracture,

A 27 ft Freightliner container being transferred from rail to road at Maiden Lane Terminal by one of the Mark 2 Drott Travelift cranes with which the early terminals were equipped. Note that unlike more modern cranes which run on rails this model moves on rubber tyres.

After dark the floodlights pick out Cardiff Terminal's two 30-ton Morris cranes built at Leicester. These are rail mounted and have the problem of being inflexible when breakdowns occur, so spares are kept at strategic places on the system. Class 56 No. No.56044 stands underneath the crane ready to haul away the overnight service to Coatbridge on 24th October 1988.

Michael J. Collins

A giant Stothert & Pitt 30-ton crane loading one of BR's cellular container ships at Harwich Parkeston Quay. These cranes have proved to be extremely reliable and can move containers 24-hours a day for weeks on end.

One of the Leyland road lorries which were used at Freightliner terminals in the 1960s. On the trailer is a 20-ton container of 1,488 cubic feet capacity.

have occurred at a number of terminals but remedial action has been taken to cure such problems.

Freightlinercare

This is a profitable sector of the activity at terminals where customer's privately owned containers can be stored and repaired. The system exploits the full depot and rail transport network to provide a national storage and positioning service for lines, agents and lessors. Full repair facilities exist at a few key locations such as Stratford and Cardiff employing skilled staff such as welders recruited from outside.

Road Fleet

Freightliner (and now Speedlink Distribution) have, ironically, one of the largest road fleets in the United Kingdom. At one time it operated 550 of its own vehicles but this figure has declined to about 300 tractor units currently with over 500 trailers. Extra vehicles can be contracted in to cope with peaks, while at other times vehicles and drivers can be contracted out. Manning is extremely flexible in the economic climate of today. A high proportion of the vehicles are capable of operating at 38 tonnes, the present maximum carrying capacity of road vehicles in the UK. Many customers prefer to undertake the collection and delivery of the containers themselves, but Freightliner do perform this service for over 40% of containers carried by the rail system. Arrangements can also be made for road movements on short to middle distance routes where the economics of rail transit is marginal.

Although Freightliner own a substantial fleet of road tractor units sometimes they are forced to buy in the services of other hauliers when trade is brisk. There is now sufficient flexibility in the system for this to happen without problems. A Guy tractor unit owned by a private haulier hauls one of Freightliner's own containers under the WCML in the London suburbs during the late 1960s. A Class 86 hauls a northbound container train overhead on the WCML.

London Terminals

It is fitting for Britain's capital city to boast four Freightliner terminals at present within the Greater Metropolitan area – two of which are the biggest and busiest on the entire system. From an operating standpoint the terminals at Stratford and Willesden play highly important roles for Railfreight Distribution, their tracks acting as hubs for the entire network. There used to be another terminal in London – again on the north side of the city – at King's Cross but this was closed at the end of 1986. Its services to Edinburgh and Newcastle (both now closed themselves) were transferred temporarily to Stratford depot. Stratford is currently by far the largest depot in London. Scheduled to start operation on 5th June 1967 it is located just outside the central zone in the north-east quarter of the metropolis. The

depot at Willesden is nearly as large and is located in the north-west of the city on the site of the former steam depot of the same name, adjacent to the WCML. The bulk of Willesden's traffic is domestic in nature while, by contrast, Stratford's traffic is mostly international in character, arriving to and from the East Coast ports.

Most trains destined for the WCML from Stratford are hauled round the North London Line by electric locomotives using the newly installed 25kV ac equipment to join the West Coast route at Camden. On arrival at Willesden

Within the confines of terminals these Douglas Tugmaster tractor units are frequently used by Freightliner to haul containers from place to place. This one is hauling a container which belongs to Canadian Pacific Ships at Cardiff terminal.

Michael J. Collins

Useful for stacking containers are these powerful Lancer Boss fork lift trucks. They are heavily ballasted at the rear and have a long wheelbase to prevent them from tipping over when carrying heavy loads.

Michael J. Collins

One of Freightliner's own Seddon Atkinson road tractor units ready to leave Cardiff Terminal with another container for local industry.

Michael J. Collins

Maiden Lane Terminal was situated alongside the North London Line near Caledonian Road station. Its rather basic facilities by today's standards were soon outstripped by the transportation demands of London's industry. In this general view taken in 1965 boxes are being unloaded from BR flat wagons. The cranes from Maiden Lane were used for some time in part of the newer Stratford Terminal.

the opportunity is often taken to add extra wagons because it is more economically viable to run as many trains as possible of the maximum 30 wagons (90TEU) for the trunk haul northwards.

Both terminals have the capacity to organise unscheduled special liner trains which can be organised at short notice to cope with large blocks of boxes. Frequently these will be made up of regular flows of maritime traffic moving on unscheduled routes, due, for example, to temporary ship diversions to different ports. Both depots have always played important roles as rail transhipment centres, in order to provide 'link' services between any two depots with no direct services. These services are kept to a minimum however, because they do create a lot of work for marginal profit levels.

From the current Freightliner timetable (Table 2, Chapter 3) it can be deduced that the two biggest London depots despatch and receive over fifty trains a day between them, or in other words, some 900 loaded wagons a day.

Officially opened on 4th August 1967 by Mr John Morris, Parliamentary Secretary, Ministry of Transport, most of Willesden's traffic has historically been domestic. Services started on 28th August 1967 with a service to and from Cardiff. Recent rationalisation of liner train services has severely curtailed traffic of this type – the shorter trunk hauls making it less able to compete with road transport. Willesden has had to rationalise its capacity, currently handling just over 200 containers a day. Stratford has few domestic routes, but enjoys a good balance of both domestic and maritime merchandise. Willesden now has a quite massive over-capacity, but its 25 acre site has been noted by Railfreight Distribution as being ideally placed to play a more important role when the Channel Tunnel is opened around 1993. Willesden also has a better depot layout when compared with Stratford. It has six main working tracks with run through access from both north and south ends and each track can hold 20 wagons. It also boasts three more single-ended tracks of 15-wagon capacity held in 'mothballs'. By contrast all ten of Stratford's gantry-served tracks are of the dead end type. Compared to Stratford, Willesden also has a very useful under-crane storage capacity. Stratford received cranes from the original York Way depot when it closed in July 1971 and these cranes formed a secondary lifting area.

One of the reasons that Stratford seems to attract so much maritime traffic is that it is sited adjacent to the major London groupage centre of London International Freight Terminal (LIFT). Prior to 1989 this enterprise was owned by 'Railfreight' but since merger with Freightliner it is operated by the combined Railfreight Distribution empire. There is, therefore a regular flow of business on Stratford

terminal's doorstep and it has its own private roadway direct into LIFT.

London's other two terminals are situated close together on industrial Thameside near Barking. Ripple Lane Terminal is the London terminus of the maritime rail network based on Southampton. Originally constructed in 1972, it was remodelled during 1974 as a centre equipped to handle company trains. It had an initial service of five inward and outward services giving capacity of 2,000 containers per week. All space on the original services was bought by three organisations under contract: Overseas Containers Ltd (OCL), Container Transportation Ltd (ACT) and the Ford Motor Company. The latter concern now takes most of its merchandise by road. Dagenham Storage, also near Barking is another private railhead operated by the large Hayes Transportation Group. It has contracts for ten wagons a day between Dagenham and Stratford to feed its containers into and out of the Railfreight Distribution system.

Non Maritime Terminals in the Midlands and North

The first terminal to be opened in Greater Birmingham – Britain's second city – was located at Dudley. Costing an initial investment of £250,000 it was opened on 6th November 1967 on the site of the former Castle goods depot. The industrial West Midlands was thriving at that time and traffic expanded rapidly. The theoretical daily throughput of containers when opened was 120 forwarded and 120 received with traffic levels soon approaching this maximum. From just 800 containers handled in 1967, the total rose to 11,600 in 1968 and then rose again to 27,900 by 1969. In its first year the weekly business went up from 113 containers to 550 and the total number handled in the first twelve months was nearly 20,000. It had three 1,000 ft long tracks and was planned to be capable of handling up to twelve container trains a day.

On the opening day the first service left at 07.45 non-stop to Glasgow and the return working arrived at 06.20 the next morning. The Glasgow run was scheduled to take less than eight hours and was formed of a 15-wagon set worked by a Class 47. A service to Newcastle started on

Right: London's other early terminal was situated at Park Royal in West London and specialised in handling traffic arriving by the GW main line from South Wales and the West Country. This night-time view shows unloading of the combined Par and Plymouth Freightliner on the first day of its operation – 11th November 1969. The combined train arrived at Park Royal just before ten o'clock each evening and returned to the West Country at 01.36. Note the 30-ton 'Rapide' crane used at this terminal.

14th November 1967 and to Stockton on 20th November. Through services to Southampton were started the following January. By the end of that month results were highly satisfactory and plans were put in hand for provision of a second West Midlands terminal. This was to be more centrally placed to handle the considerable traffic generated by the West Midlands conurbation. A new service from Dudley to Harwich Parkeston Quay was instigated on 18th March 1968 travelling via Sutton Park and Leicester. This left Dudley at 15.20 and offered greatly accelerated delivery times to Continental destinations – Zeebrugge was reached at 06.15 the next morning. The first train, unfortunately, only carried seven containers but traffic soon built up to respectable levels.

The second West Midlands terminal opened at Lawley Street, Birmingham in November 1969. It was situated about a mile east of the city centre to cater for burgeoning West Midlands traffic following the phenomenal success of Dudley. It took over services operating at that time to Belfast, Dublin, Felixstowe Docks, Harwich Parkeston Quay, London, Southampton and Tilbury. Services remaining at Dudley at that time were to Glasgow, Newcastle and Stockton.

At that time container traffic was playing a big part in the UK's export trade, often because Freightliner services were plying their trade before specialist container ships were available. BR, therefore, had an 'inland port' facility installed next door to the Lawley Street terminal which

Below: The only quiet period at Stratford Freightliner Terminal is at weekends after the Saturday morning arrivals. Class 08 No.08407 takes a well earned breather at Stratford Terminal on the Saturday afternoon of 26th February 1989.

Michael J. Collins

allowed easy cooperation with BR shipping services. The Birmingham-Harwich Parkeston Quay service would take loads of export traffic every afternoon from the heart of Birmingham to all destinations on the Continent via Zeebrugge.

The theoretical daily capacity of Lawley Street was 270 containers outwards and 270 containers inwards. Early traffic was running at about half this rate but traffic levels quickly built up with the expansion of the Freightliner network.

Unfortunately, by the 1980s the industrial decline of the West Midlands was so great that there simply was not sufficient traffic to justify two container terminals within the immediate Birmingham area. Accordingly, after much heart searching BR decided to close the Dudley terminal effective from September 1986.

The first terminal to be opened in the industrial East Midlands area was at Nottingham. It was the 22nd terminal to be opened when it was inaugurated on 30th June 1969.

It occupied an 8-acre site at Beeston which was formerly a small marshalling yard. BR awarded the £217,000 contract for its construction to O.T. Bullock & Co. Ltd and it came into operation on 30th June 1969. The terminal was equipped to process 300 containers daily and had three rail tracks together with a parallel road for collection and delivery. The first services to operate were to York Way (London) with services to Stockton-on-Tees and Newcastle following on from 7th July 1969. With the opening of Nottingham Terminal it was announced that the number of Freightliner routes had been brought up to 49. At first the terminal was quite succesful but as the economic distance for carrying containers by rail lengthened the fact that it was sited in the middle of the country went against it. After all, Nottingham was situated right on the motorway network and road competition was fierce. It did survive into the 1980s with most of its traffic being tripped to Birmingham Lawley Street for onward services, but the economic climate finally dictated that it must close in September 1986.

Just arrived at Ripple Lane (Barking) Terminal from Southampton Maritime is Class 47 No.47005 on 3rd June 1988. Note the train of empty flats on the left ready to be loaded to form a southbound working later in the day.
Michael J. Collins

Since the Par-Park Royal service was discontinued no regular Freightliner train has been booked to traverse the scenic Berks and Hants route. On 28th September 1985 however, Ripple Lane-Southampton services were diverted onto this route due to engineering works. Class 47 No.47335 runs parallel with the Kennet and Avon Canal at Great Bedwyn with a Freightliner service from Ripple Lane.

John A. M. Vaughan

Dudley Terminal's 30-ton Morris crane is visible in the background as Class 31 No.31147 in Railfreight grey livery gets the 18.30 trip working to Lawley Street under way. This terminal closed in September 1986.
Paul D. Shannon

The second West Midlands terminal at Birmingham Lawley Street under construction in early 1969.

Further north the requirements and products of the steel industry naturally provided much of Sheffield's terminal customers. It had five train routes but the most productive was the one which linked it with Cardiff and Swansea – at the centre of the country's other main steel making area. In 1971 the throughput of containers reached 500 a week. The terminal did not rely entirely on steel, other products passing through including confectionery, tobacco and glassware which travelled on the routes to Glasgow, London and Waterford, Eire. The dramatic decline in the steel industry around Sheffield eventually forced its closure.

Leeds Terminal is situated at Stourton near the site of the former steam locomotive shed south of the city on the line to Sheffield via Normanton. Opened on 31st July 1967 it was handling over 700 containers a week four years later. Maritime export and import traffic makes up a sizeable percentage of its movements so it has survived into the 1990s. The depot is situated in close proximity to the local container base (they share the same private road) and this has led to up to 80% of its throughput being destined for points overseas. It was announced in early August 1989 that, against fierce opposition from other northern centres, Leeds

The 20.15 service from Lawley Street to Felixstowe about to depart on 3rd July 1984 in the care of Class 58 No.58014. This locomotive would have worked the train as far as Nuneaton where electric traction would have taken over.

Geoff Dowling

Beeston (Nottingham) Terminal was equipped with a Morris crane and this is visible in the summer haze as Class 31 No.31167 leaves with the 15.23 service to Lawley Street on 27th July 1984. Despite having had in the past, services to London and elsewhere, this was the terminal's only remaining service at this time. It finally closed in April 1987.

Paul D. Shannon

The container depot at Hull opened on New Year's day 1968 on the site of the former Priory Yard. On the very first departure to London the train was 90% loaded – an exceptional figure for a new service. In the first ten days of its operation 116 loaded containers were despatched to London. The London service left at 19.35 and arrived at Stratford Terminal at 23.50. The return journey began at 02.30 to regain Hull at 06.38. This train was associated with haulage by the Brush prototype diesel HS4000 *Kestrel* for some months which it used to haul out and back every day. By 1971 the throughput had reached only 250 containers a week on its three routes to London, Manchester and Liverpool. Regrettably, traffic levels of this magnitude could not be sustained into the 1980s and the depot was forced to close.

The first container depot in Manchester was quite small for the size of the city and was constructed at Longsight near the electrified main line to London. By the end of 1966 consideration was being given to building a much larger facility to reflect the size of the industrial area in the immediate Manchester area. On 6th October 1969 the new terminal was opened at Trafford Park on the site of the steam shed of the same name. It was ideally placed next to the Trafford Park industrial estate and had inbuilt customs clearance for traffic which arrived by sea via the Manchester Ship Canal. The new terminal operated nightly services to South Wales, Hull and a two-section train to Stockton and Newcastle. The Manchester-Glasgow service was diverted to Trafford Park allowing Longsight to concentrate on servicing trains destined for London. The Manchester area supported the two terminals for some years but the original terminal at Longsight was eventually forced to close.

The industrial North East of England was served by the terminals at Newcastle upon Tyne and Stockton-on-Tees for many years. First to open was Newcastle which was built to serve the needs of Tyneside and Wearside. It was constructed next to the anticipated focal intersection of the new A1 road link with the Tyne Tunnel and the Newcastle-Sunderland and Newcastle-South Shields roads. It came into operation on 31st July 1967 and was visited on 27th June by the General Manager of the Eastern Region Mr Gerard Fiennes. Initially it had only one service per day to

is to get a new International Freight Terminal designed to have direct links with Europe via the Channel Tunnel. Work is due to start in 1990 and it will be sited on spare land adjacent to the container terminal. No doubt this Railfreight enterprise will bring additional prosperity to the terminal.

Class 47 No.47491 *Horwich Enterprise* backs a lengthy train of empty flats which it had brought into the Freightliner terminal at Stourton, Leeds as the 15.10 from Immingham. Illustrating the intensive use made of Freightliner wagons, these flats formed the 21.50 service through to Stratford later that evening.

Michael J. Collins

Part of the container stacking area can be seen in this view of Leeds Freightliner Terminal while Class 08 No.08661 waits its next turn of duty.

Michael J. Collins

At the start of the new timetable in May 1989 BR introduced a new Freightliner service from Leeds to Immingham. No terminal facilities are available at this port and containers have to be unloaded by crawler crane. The 11.19 Leeds FLT-Immingham service proceeds through Melton Ross, near Barnetby, on 21st August 1989 with Railfreight Distribution liveried Class 47 No.47283 *Johnnie Walker* at the head.

Michael J. Collins

For some reason photographs of Hull Freightliner Terminal are hard to come by. Fortunately this interesting view came to light of Class 20s Nos 20021 and 20208 taking a string of empty wagons under the loading crane. The brake van next to the locomotive indicates that this rake has worked recently as an unbraked set using locomotive brake power only.

Dr L. A. Nixon

and from Stratford. Remarkably, all available space on the first Southbound Stratford train had been booked by a fortnight before it actually ran! Services to and from Edinburgh, Glasgow and Birmingham were added later but the depot was a victim of the terminal closures of the 1987 profitability drive. The Stockton terminal was situated midway between Stockton and Middlesbrough and served the industrial area of Teesside.

On 16th June 1989, a brand new Freightliner terminal for Teesside was officially opened by Mr Paul Channon, Secretary of State for Transport. The new Cleveland Terminal actually opened for business on the previous 27th

February and replaced straight away the old terminal at Stockton. The new terminal was built on a site adjacent to the ICI Wilton plant – its biggest customer. The land is owned by ICI but is leased to Railfreight.

The roads between the terminal and ICI Wilton are private and are thus not subject to the rigours of the law in regard to weight restrictions. This has the advantage of allowing containers to be filled to capacity and carry a 25% bigger payload. The terminal has been designed with the needs of haulage contractors in mind and gives extremely quick lorry turnround times. It also has space for 60 rail wagons together with a stacking area used for storing up to 1,500 empty containers. Costing £2.2 million the new terminal was financed partly by an EEC grant.

Trafford Park Terminal is situated on the site of the former large steam locomotive depot of the same name. Class 87s Nos 87024 *Earl Marischal* and 87020 *North Briton* were present at the terminal on 16th January 1988.

Dr L. A. Nixon

Although the brand new Cleveland Terminal at Wilton opened for business in February 1989, BR arranged an official opening ceremony on 16th June 1989. During the ceremony the 13.51 service to Leeds departed and a specially cleaned Class 47 No.47361 *Wilton Endeavour* in new Railfreight Distribution livery was provided. Invited guests look on as the locomotive backs on to its train. Note the crane driver sitting in his console above the locomotive.

Michael J. Collins

The Maritime Terminals

The most important and busiest terminals on the present Freightliner network are the maritime terminals which serve the major ports of Britain. The earliest of these, Southampton Millbrook, was commissioned on 29th January 1968 though test trains had operated a week earlier. It presently has roughly 80% of its throughput identified as maritime and is situated on the 'up' side of the main line immediately west of Millbrook station. The tracks are served by two 30-tonne cranes. Initially its only service was the 17.39SX to Stratford returning at 04.10 from Stratford. On 5th February 1968 a second train was introduced serving Dudley Terminal and later services were introduced to Coatbridge, Barking, Leeds and Birmingham.

Southampton's second container terminal, Maritime, was opened four years later in July 1972. It was built to be contractually reserved for for OCL/ACT/Ben Line seaborne traffic to and from berths 204/206 of the docks. It is equipped to tranship up to 600 containers daily and to load or unload up to 130 Freightliner wagons in 24 hours, though this

target has been exceeded on a number of occasions. The terminal is often operational seven days a week so it is hardly surprising that this terminal had the honour of handling Freightliner's millionth container during May 1972. It was discharged from a Japanese vessel for onward transport to Barking Terminal. The terminal is situated on the 'down' side of the line between Millbrook and Redbridge stations and is a larger yard than Millbrook, covering over 30 acres.

Tilbury Terminal was opened during 1970 on the site of the former exchange sidings between the Port of London Authority (PLA) lines and the BR Barking-Tilbury line. The terminal plan was different from the other terminals then existing in that no facilities were envisaged for the storage of containers near to the terminal itself, except for any parking that may be necessary during loading or unloading. All containers were to be conveyed to and from ship's berths or to storage spaces adjacent to the berths which could be up to two miles away.

Tilbury Terminal consists of a four-lane roadway and two sidings spanned by a 30-ton 6-wheel container crane. The

A view of the 35-ton Stothert & Pitt cantilever crane loading a container train at Southampton Maritime Freightliner Terminal soon after building.

A more up to date photograph of Southampton Maritime Terminal. On a very rainy 10th February 1990 Class 47 No.47052, in correct Railfreight Distribution livery, backs a train of empty flats into the terminal. In the left background a Class 442 emu passes with a Waterloo to Poole express.

Michael J. Collins

sidings lead in at the north via BR's Seabrook sidings near Grays. Within a month of opening the terminal was handling over 1,000 containers per week.

In 1978 the Northfleet Hope Terminal was opened within the Tilbury Container Services Ltd complex. This is locally referred to as the "mini terminal" and was purchased by OCL. On completion it was handed over to Tilbury Container Services to operate. The significance of this is that at Tilbury there are essentially two Freightliner operations: the primary rail container depot site where main line trains collect and despatch containers and the mini terminal from where other trains are tripped down to the main site. An interesting train which emanates from the mini terminal is one which handles movements of Anchor Butter from New Zealand which is transported on a special train via Stratford to their cold storage centre at Swindon. In 1987 3,695 containers full of butter were transported – about 300 million half pound pack equivalents!

Further northwards up the east coast are sited a whole cluster of container depots on the Orwell Estuary. The most significant is the Port of Felixstowe which has enjoyed phenomenal success over recent years due to its ideal

One of the earliest terminals on the SR system was Southampton Millbrook which was commissioned in 1968. A good view of the two cranes is obtainable in this shot of Class 47 No.47107 which has just been detached from the 08.10 SO arrival from Willesden on 10th February 1990. The locomotive will now be stabled for the weekend at the nearby Eastleigh Traction Maintenance Depot.

Michael J. Collins

Although built in 1970 next to the electrified Fenchurch Street-Shoeburyness line, it was not until nearly twenty years later that the overhead catenary was extended into Tilbury Terminal to allow through running of electric locomotives on trains from the north. Standing under the wires with the crane in the background is Class 47 No.47407 which had arrived with the overnight service from Leeds and was preparing to return to Ripple Lane Traction Depot for weekend stabling towing a string of empties.

Michael J. Collins

Causing excitement amongst the local population at Tilbury on 10th October 1988 was the arrival at the Freightliner terminal of preserved LNER Class A3 Pacific No.4472 *Flying Scotsman*. The next day she was loaded on board ship for the long voyage to Australia to haul a number of special tours 'down under'.

Michael J. Collins

The new Felixstowe North Terminal was officially opened on 2nd March 1987. To mark the occasion a special passenger train had been brought down the branch from Trimley to convey visiting dignitaries. Class 47s Nos 47585 *County of Cambridgeshire* and 47291 (named *Port of Felixstowe* that day) topped and tailed the special train seen parked opposite the new terminal.

John A. Day

Felixstowe North Terminal in business on 13th June 1988. On the left stands Class 37s Nos 37358 *P & O Containers* and 37011 with the 18.15 departure to Coatbridge. Under the gantry can be seen class 37s Nos 37004 and 37055 with the 19.30 departure for Stratford.
Michael J. Collins

A train load of Ford Motor Co. components from Halewood bound for Genk, Belgium, arrives at Harwich Parkeston Quay on 20th August 1968. Providing traction is two-tone green liveried Class 47 No.D1779.

position and freedom from labour troubles. All of the port area including the rail container terminals is owned by the Felixstowe Dock & Railway Company which was incorporated in 1875. There is a very close relationship with BR however, and the first rail-served container terminal for the port was opened in the Landguard area of the docks in 1972. At first Freightliner trains had to proceed into the Felixstowe station area in order to run round and gain access to the docks. On 13th May 1970 a 650 yard spur was re-opened which allowed direct running into the docks without reversal. The spur followed the original alignment direct to the docks via Felixstowe Beach first opened in 1877. It had been closed in 1898. The original terminal was complemented in May 1987 with the opening of a second terminal, Felixstowe North, the original terminal then

becoming known as Felixstowe South. The new terminal was situated adjacent to the Walton, Dooley and Trinity container terminals. This involved the construction of a new single track rail spur from the Felixstowe branch at Trimley, down to the new terminal. The line was the first brand new piece of railway opened on a green field site anywhere in the UK for many years. This saved routing Freightliner trains through the dock complex. Here lengthy delays to road traffic was becoming frustrating, causing much congestion as trains crossed over a number of closely spaced level crossings.

At Felixstowe there is a strong liaison between the two operating companies which ensures that a top quality service is maintained for customers. Growth has been incredible and a massive 180,000 TEUs were handled by

At Harwich Parkeston Quay is Class 08 No.08498 shunting a string of wagons which had arrived as a trip from Ipswich after being detached from a train from Willesden on 26th February 1989. Parkeston Quay was temporarily closed to rail borne container traffic during 1987/1988 but had reopened again shortly before this photograph was taken.
Michael J. Collins

Access to Ipswich Griffin Wharf Freightliner Terminal is gained by a short spur diverging from the GE main line at Halifax Junction, south of Ipswich. Just arriving with a train of Seawheel containers bearing steel coil from South Wales is local Class 08 No.08407 during August 1988.
Michael J. Collins

Freightliner in 1987. Daily services leave Felixstowe direct to Birmingham, Bristol, Cardiff, Coatbridge, Glasgow, Holyhead (for shipping links to Belfast and Dublin), Leeds, London (Stratford and Willesden), Liverpool and Manchester. All these services are available in the reverse direction and there is a daily capacity for an export/import throughput of 1,200 TEUs. An important addition to the range of services at Felixstowe occurred in December 1985 when Freightliner transferred its Continental Europe import/export distribution service to the Felixstowe-Zeebrugge short sea route instead of using Harwich. The shipping leg of this service operated six days a week – in each direction – via two purpose-built cellular vessels with capacity for 320 TEUs. Surprisingly however, Felixstowe does not rely purely on trade with the near-Continent. It is a port of true international flavour with many containers arriving from both North American and Far Eastern ports of origin.

Facing Felixstowe on the southern bank of the Orwell is Harwich Parkeston Quay. This was the first container depot designed to project the Freightliner network into Continental Europe. It was from here that BR commercially launched their international container scheme between Harwich and Zeebrugge on 18th March 1968 after an £8 million two-year construction scheme. It was heralded as a "showpiece which we expect people will come from all over the world to see," by Mr Stanley Raymond, Chairman of the BRB at the opening ceremony. In the initial stages traffic actually had to be suppressed because only half the cranes were commissioned at that time, and neither at Parkeston nor Zeebrugge was the full length of the quay available. These restraints only lasted for a very short time however, and late in July 1968 a full service began. By the end of that year the operation was working at the rate of 50,000 – 60,000 container movements a year.

Harwich was the destination of the first 'company' Freightliner container train from the Ford Motor Company plant at Halewood via the Harwich-Zeebrugge service to their Belgian plant. It maintained a rail borne conveyor belt of components between the two factories.

Ipswich, further up the Orwell, is used as a convenient point for splitting and reforming container trains arriving from and destined for both Felixstowe and Harwich. A number of trains arrive here direct from Willesden with a portion travelling on to Felixstowe and another portion travelling for a few miles back on itself until it reaches Manningtree, junction for the Harwich branch. In addition to this the port of Ipswich boasts two container terminals itself, one on the north bank of the river at Cliff Quay and another on the opposite bank at Griffin Wharf. Both of these terminals generate at least one train a day sometimes more. A considerable tonnage of Fyffes bananas arrive in the UK at Ipswich's Cliff Quay Terminal whilst Griffin Wharf specialises in steel coil traffic amongst other cargo.

Maritime terminals on the west side of Britain are not quite so numerous. Liverpool is served by the major terminal at Garston which was enlarged to twice its size during October 1969. After the rebuilding was completed services to Southampton and Hull were added to the existing trains to London (2), Glasgow, Cardiff, Swansea, Stockton and

Newcastle. In early September 1981 the 10 millionth container to be carried by Freightliner began its rail leg from Garston Terminal. The container carried medical supplies from the Glaxo laboratory at Speke for distribution in South East England. To mark the occasion, the BR Chairman, Sir Peter Parker presented the Glaxo factory manager with a framed citation. In 1978 the Department of Transport made a Section 8 grant of £412,000 towards the cost of a new Freightliner terminal at Royal Seaforth Dock, Liverpool. This covered half of the cost of the terminal which was constructed in order to provide a link between the Port of Liverpool's Royal Seaforth maritime container terminal and the BR container network. An initial service of two trains a day started in summer 1979.

After a brief flirtation with the port of Heysham BR now sees the port of Holyhead as the focus of its Irish operations. When announced, it was heralded as a £7.5 million scheme to project the Freightliner network into Ireland. Hand in hand with the Holyhead development and included in the price was the development of terminal facilities and quayside cranes at both Dublin and Belfast. Research had shown that the Irish Sea operation had to be concentrated on just one English port. Holyhead was chosen because from here the sea passages to Belfast as well as Dublin are shorter than from either Liverpool or Heysham. At that time the Chester-Holyhead main line was not on a good financial footing and this terminal tipped the economic balance and dispelled any anxiety about the future of the line.

Traffic to and from Holyhead was severely disrupted when the Menai Bridge was severely damaged by fire on

A new terminal was opened at Seaforth in the heart of the Liverpool docklands in 1978 with the aid of government finance. This terminal complements the other Liverpool terminal at Garston rather than competing with it. Passing Alexandra Dock, Class 47 No.47380 halts road traffic as it crosses the main road on its way down the Seaforth branch with a loaded container train on 2nd April 1986.

Paul D. Shannon

The 15.05 Freightliner departure to Crewe Basford Hall gets under way from Holyhead on 17th April 1985 behind Class 47 No.47106. The terminal facilities and container storage area can be seen in the background.

Paul D. Shannon

On 3rd May 1976 a fire severely damaged the Menai Bridge making it impossible for trains to cross into Anglesey until it was repaired. A number of traction units were marooned at Holyhead and had to be shipped back to the mainland. A temporary Freightliner terminal was used at Caernarvon for Dublin traffic only. Class 47 No.D1818 arrives with a container train on 1st January 1971.

A. Wyn Hobson

An early view of Cardiff Terminal showing the original 30-ton Allen crane taking a 20 ft container from a train.

3rd May 1970. A temporary container depot was opened at Caernarvon during the currency of the emergency. During the crisis Holyhead/Caernarvon only dealt with the container traffic to and from Dublin, as the traffic to Belfast was temporarily served by the facilities at Heysham Harbour. Containers were roaded from Caernarvon to Holyhead for shipment at this time and the extra road working between rail and ship over approximately 30 miles must have been extremely expensive. Traffic was allowed to increase again after the Menai Bridge was re-opened to traffic in 1972. In the financial year ending 31st March 1988 Freightliner notched up record volumes on its daily services between Britain and Eire. For that year 35,616 containers were carried. Harp Lager, Goodyear and Kimberley Clark were just some of the famous names featured in this traffic.

In February 1970 plans were unveiled for a £10.5 million project to build a deep-sea container port at Falmouth. The scheme was aimed at the second generation of container ships and the concept was designed to cater for 40,000 tonnes deadweight vessels with a container carrying capacity of over 3,000 containers. The premise used was that highly attractive economics of ship utilisation could be enjoyed if ships crossing the Atlantic or arriving from the Mediterranean could transfer their cargo in the far South West instead of continuing onwards to Southampton or Tilbury. Unfortunately, the plan never materialised but rumours occasionally surface today of plans to proceed with the scheme.

Class 25s Nos 25313 and 25072 shunting Cardiff terminal on 9th June 1982.

Colin J. Marsden

Empty Seawheel containers from Cardiff Terminal approach the giant British Steel Corporation plant at Llanwern on 27th August 1987 behind Class 47 No.47376. The containers will be filled with steel coil in the works and sent for export via Ipswich Griffin Wharf the next day.

Michael J. Collins

Non Maritime Terminals in Wales and the West

The only terminal remaining in South Wales in the current network is at Cardiff. It is situated on a 10-acre site at Pengam, two miles east of Cardiff, on the site of a former Great Western Railway goods yard. The depot commenced operations in June 1967 and was opened by Mrs Barbara Castle, then Minister of Transport. The first service to operate from the depot was a combined Manchester and Liverpool train which began running from 30 June. The London service began operating from 31st July 1967.

The throughput at Cardiff is currently around 32,000 containers a year. At present the depot has two daily outward services, one to Coatbridge and Holyhead which splits at Crewe, and another to Stratford which carries containers for onward transit to Ipswich and Felixstowe. The depot is also called on to handle a number of specials to the East Coast ports from the British Steel Company (BSC) steelworks at Llanwern and Port Talbot. Cardiff is also involved in the movement of southbound Alcan aluminium slab from the plants at Lynemouth (Northumberland) and Fort William using the Railfreight Distribution networks. This activity is particularly interesting and unusual in the context of this

Under a threatening sky Class 47 No.47245 passes Margam with an Eastbound Freightliner from the now closed terminal at Danygraig (Swansea).

Dr L. A. Nixon

It was certainly unusual to find Construction sub-sector Class 56 No. 56001 *Whatley* at Bristol West Depot on a Freightliner train. The working is the 13.50 West Depot-Gloucester of 13th November 1989. This runs as a mixed container and 'Speedlink' train and the Freightliner wagons are detached at Gloucester and attached to the Cardiff-Coatbridge service at that point.

Mike Goodfield

book. An average of 20-25 containers, each containing two or three slabs weighing six tonnes are delivered to the British Aluminium plant at Rogerstone from Pengam each day. After rolling, these slabs leave as coils on the northbound service to Coatbridge for onward transit to Falkirk where they are used to produce a variety of finished products such as foil, bottle tops and wrappings.

The Cardiff depot also has an active interest at Swindon Yard some 80 miles away. Here a supervisor and six road vehicles are employed to deliver the Anchor butter which arrives by container train from Tilbury. It is taken from Swindon Yard to Anchor's warehouse and cold storage centre which is situated nearby. This exercise calls for a vehicle to arrive at the warehouse every 15 minutes precisely so that the packaging conveyor is fed at the correct rate.

The other terminal in South Wales at Swansea (Danygraig) came into operation on 24th February 1969. It

In pouring rain Class 86/4 No.86402 working in multiple with Class 87 No.87035 Robert Burns *prepare to leave Coatbridge Terminal with the 19.40 service to Stratford.*
Maxwell H. Fowler

On 13th August 1983 Class 37 No.37011 pilots Class 20 No.20043 on empty container wagons from the Clyde container base in Greenock destined for Glasgow Freightliner Terminal. The train was photographed west of Bishopton.
Tom Noble

had daily services to and from Sheffield, Willesden and Harwich Parkeston Quay. It was the 21st terminal to be opened in the UK and at first business was good. It was forced to close however, from April 1987 as part of Freightliners profitability drive following disastrous profit margins the previous year.

Since the closure of Swansea Depot the Cardiff terminal now has the responsibility for the flow of raw materials from Felixstowe to the giant International Nickel works nearby. Cardiff also operates a night trunking operation for keg beer traffic to the Scottish and Newcastle Brewery and for the Post Office in addition to the standard work undertaken for a number of major customers such as the Royal Mint and Seawheel.

The Freightliner depot at Bristol is situated opposite the West Depot carriage sidings on the West of England main line on the 'down' side of Parsons Street station. It attracts considerable container traffic from Avonmouth Docks and Bristol's own Portbury Dock. At present it has services to and from Coatbridge and Stratford. When Freightliner merged with 'Speedlink' in 1988, Bristol was the first depot to run a mixed train of Freightliner stock and ordinary air-braked freight vehicles under the new arrangements which were then possible.

Scottish Terminals

The first terminal to open in Scotland was at Glasgow and was the destination of the very first Freightliner train. Located at Gushetfaulds it attained a 20% payload within three weeks of the opening of the Glasgow – London service and this was viewed as a reasonable achievement at this time. By Summer 1967 the depot was handling some 900 containers a week – half of all BR's Freightliner traffic! A second terminal serving Glasgow is now sited at Coatbridge, Strathclyde near the M74 motorway. Although the terminal was officially opened in 1976 by the Secretary of State for Scotland, there had been a Freightliner presence

Class 37 No. 37072 shunts a rake of Freightliner empties at Clydeport, Greenock on 15th June 1985.

George C. O'Hara

The 06.10 Glasgow to Aberdeen Freightliner crosses the Montrose Basin on 30th March 1974 hauled by Class 47 No.1918.

Brian Morrison

since 1970. In those early days there was only one service in each direction to and from the East Coast ports of Tilbury, Felixstowe and Harwich. Now there are services to Southampton (2), Liverpool, Felixstowe (2), Glasgow (2), a combined Birmingham/Cardiff train and a combined Willesden/Stratford train. At one time there were services to Aberdeen, Nottingham and Hull before closure of these depots. In financial terms the principal cargo handled at Coatbridge is whisky – in 1974, 9 million gallons left for Japan alone!

All other Scottish Freightliner terminals are now closed. Edinburgh, Dundee, Aberdeen and Greenock have all fallen victim to economic cuts. The Edinburgh terminal was built on the site of the engineer's depot at Portobello and completed stage one of the Freightliner network. Opened on 8th January 1968 it initially operated a service to Stratford Terminal because it was expected that large quantities of whisky would be handled and this would connect with the London-Paris and Harwich-Zeebrugge workings. The first London working included a 20 feet container of Vat 69 from William Sanderson of Leith destined for Paris. In later years the Edinburgh trains were diverted to King's Cross before that depot closed and trains ran for a brief period to Stratford again before Edinburgh Terminal itself was closed.

The Aberdeen to London service, at 523 miles was the longest on the entire Freightliner system. The Aberdeen terminal was the second depot to be opened in Scotland. It joined the network from October 1966 and was hurried into operation ahead of its planned stage in the national programme to safeguard a vital meat contract. William Donald were threatening to transfer their lucrative London business to road haulage unless BR could offer them a modern high-capacity container service. This firm had privately-owned insulated containers (with an identifying bull's head logo) for its consignments of meat destined for the Sainsbury supermarket chain. The firm was the keystone of the 60% load factor which the Aberdeen-London trains soon built up. The reverse train struggled at first to a 30% load factor. The train schedules were drawn up with the aim of meeting the marketing needs of the fresh meat trades London market requirements. In the 1960s Freightliner were hopeful of gaining some of the fish trade for Aberdeen Terminal but this did not materialise in bulk, falling victim to the number of small Aberdeen road hauliers whose keen prices significantly undercut the Freightliner rates. Aberdeen was the first depot to boast a six days a week service on the London run but it was forced to revert back to five days a week operation from August 1968. Paper mills in the vicinity of Aberdeen were an early customer but certain sizes of reel did not sit happily in Freightliner containers and ultimately the traffic was lost.

Class 47 No.47117 heads the 14.10 Aberdeen-Glasgow past Hilton Junction, Perth, on 20th July 1984.

Paul D. Shannon

Mixed Trains

In contrast to the late 1980s, earlier in the decade it was a common sight to see Freightliner rakes incorporated in trains of ordinary air-braked freight vehicles. A train typical of the time is exemplified by this 'up' Saturday morning service heading for Harwich Parkeston Quay past Ely behind Class 37 No.37041 on 13th March 1982. Notice the 'Campbells Soups' PVA coupled immediately behind the locomotive and the Freightliner 5-set following on behind it.

Michael J. Collins

Class 46 No.46023 passing Dr Day's Bridge Junction, Bristol, on 8th July 1975 with a mixed freight train bound for Scotland. A Freightliner set has been marshalled towards the rear of the train – a common practice in the 1970s.

Terry Nicholls

The 16.55 Harwich Parkeston Quay-Halewood 'company' Freightliner is seen approaching Witham, Essex, on 16th May 1980 behind Class 47 No.47332. Two German VTG Cargo waggons are coupled immediately behind the locomotive.

Michael J. Collins

On 15th April 1983 Class 37 No.37138 snarls up Belstead Bank, south of Ipswich, with the very heavy 23.35 Mossend-Parkeston Quay air-braked freight. A Freightliner set is marshalled in the middle of the train. Shortly after this picture was taken it became rare to see Freightliner sets in ordinary freight services.

Michael J. Collins

When Freightliner and Speedlink were merged in Autumn 1988 to form 'Railfreight Distribution' it became common again to see mixed freight trains including Freightliners. Some trains were in fact booked to run thus. A very scruffy Class 37, No.37242 in two-tone Railfreight livery bearing 'Railfreight Distribution' decals stands in Ipswich Yard at the head of three oil tanks and a Freightliner rake forming a service to Parkeston Quay on 20th January 1990.

Michael J. Collins

Anglo-Scottish Traffic

Class 85 No.85018 passes Norton Bridge, Staffordshire, with a well loaded Glasgow-Stratford Freightliner on 26th April 1986.

John Whitehouse

Framed in a bridge arch at Fenny Compton the 07.10 Coatbridge-Southampton service has notable power in the form of Class 56 No.56089 on 28th July 1984.

John C. Baker

Within half a mile of Shap Summit in the early morning of 1st June 1989 is Class 86 No.86403 together with Class 87 No.87030 *Black Douglas* at the head of the 02.04 MSX Willesden-Glasgow service. These two locomotives can operate in multiple because they are fitted with the necessary multiple working equipment. No doubt the class 87 has worked right through from London but it is likely that the Class 86/4 was attached at Crewe to assist over the northern fells.

Michael J. Collins

Leaving Aberdeen for London is Class 47 No. 47208 seen passing Craiginches on 2nd September 1977. Until closure of Aberdeen Terminal this was the longest mileage of any regular Freightliner.

Dr L. A. Nixon

Passing rows of terraced housing so typical of the industrial North East of England, the 19.05 Stockton-Coatbridge Freightliner recorded passing Eaglescliffe, Cleveland, on 19th May 1982. Judging from the empty flatwagons behind the locomotive, No.47052, business does not appear to have been too brisk on this service at the time.

Colin J. Marsden

The 18.45 Dudley-Glasgow service approaching Wednesbury on 29th May 1986 with Class 47 No.47060 in charge. The photograph was taken from the embankment of the former ex-GWR main line from Wolverhampton to Birmingham Snow Hill. The track diverging right from under the rear of the locomotive is the last remains of the Princes End branch.

Geoff Dowling

CHAPTER 6

Freightliner Cabride

An invitation from Railfreight to ride on a Freightliner train found the author at Ipswich station on Wednesday 29th August 1988 at lunch time. In the Station Supervisor's office I found Traction Inspector Bob Clow, who was to accompany me, ready and waiting. We chatted as we walked along to Ipswich Yard by way of the authorised walking route. He told me that he had joined the railway at Harwich Parkeston Quay in the days of steam and had fired and driven all the steam locomotive types associated with the ex-Great Eastern lines – 'Sandringhams', 'Britannias', B1s, K3s – the lot. Dieselisation in the late 1950s and early 1960s led to him doing conversion courses on all diesel types and he had in time risen through the ranks to attain the position of Traction Inspector.

There are usually a number of Freightliner trains on view at Ipswich Yard and today was no exception. As we entered

Ipswich station on 29th August 1988 as Class 08 No.08464 passes through the station with the 11.30 Freightliner trip from Griffin Wharf to Ipswich Yard including a 5-set destined for Birmingham. This set was attached to the train on which the author rode at Ipswich Yard. On the right Class 156 'Sprinter' No.156417 is ready to depart with a train from Harwich Parkeston Quay – also destined for Birmingham!

Michael J. Collins

the yard by the path near the staff amenity block, a pair of Class 37s rasped into life and drew a long Freightliner train out of the yard and headed south up the main line. Also in the yard was the Ipswich pilot, No.08708, together with Class 47 No.47440 stabled nearby. Our train had started at Felixstowe earlier at 10.15 as a service to Willesden but had stopped at Ipswich Yard for extra traffic to be added. Our locomotive from Ipswich to Willesden was to be Class 47 No.47590 *Thomas Telford* which on this occasion, looked rather scruffy in travel weary rail blue livery. As we approached the locomotive was shunting a five set of 'CAST' and 'Seawheel' containers onto our train. This set had arrived from Griffin Wharf – one of the two terminals which serve this busy East Coast port. Our guard, Mr Trimingham, was accompanied by a trainee guard and both would be riding in the rear cab of the locomotive. They were busy carrying out the usual brake tests. This completed we were informed that our train would leave at 12.50. The train had been marshalled by a local driver and he climbed down from the cab to hand over to Dave Guinea who had just arrived and was to be our driver on this trip. Dave, too, proved to be a very experienced man. He had been on the footplate for no less than 35 years – 22 of them at Stratford Depot in East

A rear view of the 11.30 Freightliner trip from Ipswich Griffin wharf showing the brake van, No. B955087, attached at the rear. This is done because the train has to be propelled along the Griffin Wharf branch until it reverses direction on the GE main line at Halifax Junction.

Michael J. Collins

London. We learned that the complete train was made up of 25 wagons divided into five sets of five wagons. There was only nine empty container spaces on the train and thus it was regarded as being well loaded and, indeed, would be quite a handful for a single Class 47. Behind the locomotive the first five-set was 4M47 containing 372 tonnes for Birmingham. Behind this was 4M42 a second five-set containing 243 tonnes for London. Following was 4M81 a five-set containing 130 tonnes for Holyhead and finally was the ten-set 4M81 containing 347 tonnes destined for Coatbridge. Our train would need substantial rearrangement on arrival at Willesden.

Just before departure time Dave walked the length of the train and inspected each wagon for potential problems as he passed. He was particularly concerned that the couplings and brake connections were in good order before taking charge of the train. At 12.52 a Freightliner set destined for the West Bank Terminal passed us behind Class 08 No.08464. Bob explained that this working was interesting as it usually conveys a brake van because it sometimes runs along the quay, beside the River Orwell as a loose-coupled train. Today was no exception and a red and grey CAR type brake van brought up the rear. Bob recognised the driver of the train as Peter Parsley, an Ipswich man, and he was given a cheery greeting as he passed. As we stood talking, Class 47 No.47156 arrived at Ipswich Yard from the south with the daily 'Speedlink' working from Willesden. The payload of just one tank wagon could not have attracted much revenue on this particular day.

A heave up the metal rungs and through a door of prac-

tical width and I found myself in the spacious cab of No. 47590. Two padded armchairs are provided for the crew and Inspector Clow invited me to sit in the one on the second man's side. Dave, the driver, explained that he had been on this turn all week. On Monday, the train had been loaded to ten wagons, on Tuesday to 15 and today we had ten more. In front of him Dave had the usual gauges to watch – speed, amps, oil and air pressure together with several warning lamps configured into a neat binnacle. Four handles make up the controls of a Class 47 – one for power, a reverser and two brake handles, one for vacuum and one for air brakes. The vacuum brake would not be needed on this run.

At 13.01 we received permission to proceed and Dave opened up the power handle. The twelve cylinders of the Sulzer LDA-28C engine began to make their presence heard as well as felt as No.47590 started to get the Freightliner train on the move. On the ammeter power was steady at 2,000 amps as we crept through the yard. Dave followed trainmens' regulations and poked his head out of the cab and looked rearwards to ensure that our load was trailing correctly. Approaching the station Dave allowed the power output to increase to 4,000 amps and we passed the station in the centre through road. Stabled in the yard were Class 37s Nos 37144 and 37251 and as we passed a couple of train spotters noted down our number. Waiting in the station was a Felixstowe bound dmu with Class 101 Nos 54347 + 51201 forming the train. A green light on the station footbridge signal allowed Dave to pull the power handle right over to give the locomotive its head. A roar emanated from behind as No.47590 began to accelerate the heavy train ready for the assault of Belstead Bank just beyond Ipswich. We plunged into Ipswich Tunnel with the instrument panel glowing. The locomotive headlight illuminated our way and although it was high summer, large drips of water rained down from the tunnel ceiling. Daylight gradually approached and we burst out of the tunnel at 30mph with 4,000 amps showing on the ammeter. On our left we passed the wagon repair shops and remains of the former Ipswich steam depot which still stands. A large number of empty Freightliner flats were awaiting attention in the repair shops. Soon we passed Halifax Junction where the branch down to the docks at Griffin Wharf diverges.

The continuous rating of a Class 47 is 4,200 amps and we were just fractionally under this figure as full power was applied at the foot of Belstead Bank. In view on the left was the new Orwell Bridge used by hundreds of road wagons every day taking containers to Felixstowe Docks. Our speed at this point was 37 mph and Dave successfully held this speed in order to keep the locomotive in the first stage of weak field. This ensured that the maximum tractive effort was available for hill climbing. As we surmounted the summit at 13.12 the ammeter momentarilly slipped over to 8,000 amps and the second stage of field diversion came in automatically. As we commenced the descent to Bentley Bank the train began to pick up speed but the ride in the cab was quite steady. Dave eased back the power handle because sufficient acceleration would be given to the train solely by the falling gradient. As we passed the remains of Bentley station (the one-time junction for the Hadleigh branch) speed had risen to 55 mph and the locomotive was comfortably in command of the train. Speed had reached 60 mph as we swept downhill to approach the Essex/Suffolk border at the bridge over the Suffolk Stour just east of Manningtree. Dave gave a warning toot on the horn as we approached the bridge because men were seen working on the track. At Manningtree North Junction we passed another Class 47 heading north on the Parkeston-Mossend 'Speedlink' freight and Bob Clow gave a friendly wave to Driver Ken Sylvan who was at the controls. Bob seemed to know everybody who works on the GE main line!

Green signals at Manningtree station and Dave opened up the power handle for the ascent of Dedham Bank. Dave remarked that there used to be a signal box on the bank on the 'up' side. As we forged up the bank with 5,000 amps indicated Dave and Bob started reminiscing about the days of steam. Bob pretended that he was firing a B12 and knocked on the water feed and shovelled a few more lumps of coal into the firebox! Approaching Colchester North speed was at 50 mph and increased to 65 mph as we descended the bank at the junction with the Clacton line. We passed the station at this speed and in the blur I noticed Class 313 emu No.313099 filling up with passengers for yet another trip down to Clacton via St Botolphs. A Class 312 was in the 'down' platform on a stopping train to Ipswich. It was school holidays and the inevitable group of train spotters noted our number as we swept past the locomotive servicing depot. Situated on the 'up' side of the line

just south of Colchester station the depot was purpose-built in the early days of dieselisation. Today it held the protoype Class 37 No. 37350 (D6700) resplendent in green livery, together with Nos 37073 and 37087 and a couple of shunters.

As we passed, Dave kept the power handle open for the ascent of Stanway Bank. One of the features of the GE main line is these short, but quite steep, banks which keep enginemen on their toes. Speed was 62 mph at the bottom of the bank with power output steady at 4,000 amps. As we crossed the River Colne by the high viaduct a combined harvester was at work on the wheat crop below us and a Class 309 emu passed us on a Liverpool Street-Clacton fast train. We laboured up the bank and as we passed the remains of Stanway sidings speed had decreased to 50 mph with power output up at 4,200 amps. The heavy load behind us was taking its toll and the massive Sulzer engine was working hard. Just north of Marks Tey we passed the late running Class 86 hauled 12.30 Liverpool Street-Norwich express held at the signals to the north of the yard. Marks Tey Yard is the loading point for a daily sand train which runs down to Mile End, East London, but today the sidings were empty apart from a tipper lorry discharging its load of sand from one of the nearby pits. Marks Tey Yard signal box still survives as do one or two semaphore signals controlling access to the yards. Manual signals are quite rare on electrified track. As we powered through the station a track machine was ready to start work on the Sudbury branch.

We now entered a long stretch of fairly straight gently

Stratford driver Dave Guinea at the controls of Class 47 No.47590 *Thomas Telford.*

Michael J. Collins

Class 47 No.47590 *Thomas Telford* at the head of the 12.50 Freightliner departure from Ipswich Yard to Willesden on 29th August 1989. The working had originated at Felixstowe South earlier in the day. On the right Class 08 No.08464 is ready to take an empty 5-set down to Ipswich West Bank Terminal.

Michael J. Collins

undulating track. Just before Kelvedon station Dave was not touching any of the controls excepting the dead man's handle. Bob remarked that the locomotive was quite capable of looking after itself on track like this. It was not likely to pick up sufficient speed to break any speed limits with this heavy load and it would be quite happy to continue in this way until we reached Chelmsford where we would have to slow for the slack through the station. Dave was taking a well earned breather and was simply watching the signals and admiring the scenery as we rolled through the Essex agricultural countryside. On the approaches to Kelvedon station there is a slight left hand curve and I was asked to look round the corner from my seat to see if anyone was on the track and to give them a hoot up. Unfortunately no one was there! We were now on one of the fastest stretches of the GE main line which is passed for 100 mph operation by expresses at this point. We powered through Witham station passing another Class 312 emu in the Braintree branch platform. Beyond Hatfield Peverel station the railway runs parallel to the busy A12 dual carriageway for some miles and we showed a clean pair of heels to all the lorries heading south. Men were working on the track at the site of the one-time New Hall loop as we approached this point.

We then descended the quite steep bank east of Chelmsford until we crossed the River Chelmer and entered Chelmsford station. There is a permanent speed restriction of 60 mph through the curved platforms of Chelmsford station and we passed at exactly the correct speed. In Chelmsford Yard we noticed one of the electric parcels units, No.308995, unloading another quantity of mail destined for the Essex county town. The signal box is extant at Chelmsford situated on the 'down' side of the line high above the station awnings and platforms. Yet another Class 312 emu, forming a Witham service from Liverpool Street, was disgorging passengers as we passed. Just north of Chelmsford station the automatic warning system fitted in the cab of No.47590 gave the first buzzer of the trip, signifying a signal with an aspect other than green ahead and Dave eased off the power. As we passed on the viaduct, high over Chelmsford, people were enjoying themselves fishing and passing the time of day in the park. We noticed Chelmsford City football ground on the left and the enormous Marconi Radar plant on the other side of the track. One or two people working in their offices stopped what they were doing and had a look as we swept majestically by with our massive trailing load. A signal ahead displayed a double-yellow aspect accounting for the buzzer heard on the AWS. This section of line was electrified just after World War II and we noted the older type catenary carrying the overhead lines. Class 309 emu No.309027 flashed past us as we powered our way up the short bank out of Chelmsford with a power output of 4,200 amps.

Ingatestone station was passed at 13.57 and 48 mph and we all gave a wave to the crossing keeper as we swept by. We were just about right time and Dave and Bob thought it highly likely that we would be looped at Shenfield in order that faster traffic behind us could pass. A Class 86 flashed past us on the 'down' road with 13.30 Liverpool

Street-Norwich. Shenfield signal U22 was showing a yellow aspect and the cab buzzer sounded. Dave shut off engine power and applied the brakes. I heard the air pump, situated behind me in the engine compartment chatter into life to keep a head of compressed air for braking. A red aspect was showing on signal 78 as we approached Shenfield station. As we approached very slowly the feather went off to take us round the back of the station. Dave applied more power and the locomotive struggled to get its heavy train rolling again. The Sulzer engine throbbed behind us as the power output surged up to 6,000 amps just for a moment. As we slowly traversed the loop a railman sweeping the station platform stopped for a few seconds to watch our progress. We proceeded through the station and on to the summit of Brentwood Bank where we drew to a halt. After a couple of minutes Class 309 No.309606 sped past us on a Clacton-Liverpool Street express. After a few seconds we received a green light and Dave eased on the power to get our train back into motion and we were given the 'up' main line. The train accelerated quickly down Brentwood Bank with gravity assistance and approaching Brentwood station Dave shut off power and gave a gentle touch of the brakes to control speed. A 30 mph temporary speed restriction just beyond the station impeded our progress and Dave had to let the entire train pass through – not just the engine – before we could accelerate away again. We crossed the M25 motorway at 14.15 and began to roll our way through the London suburbs. Rail traffic was brisk with a succession of emu operated trains passing on all lines.

At Harold Wood No.47590 began to judder and shake alarmingly as we rolled along. Dave said that it was nothing to worry about. He had found the 'flat spot' on the power handle and every single Class 47 has this characteristic when the power handle is placed at this particular position. Dave wound the power handle back and the juddering stopped immediately and we rolled downhill at a steady 60 mph with no power being taken from the engine at all.

Passing Gidea Park there was a number of Class 315 emus stabled in the sidings awaiting use in the evening rush hour which would soon start. During the morning and evening peaks, line occupation is heavy because of commuter traffic and freight movements are banned except in circumstances of extreme emergency, but we would beat the ban easily on this working. As we passed through the bridge at the south end of Gidea Park station at 45 mph a couple of youngsters suddenly appeared on the track right in front of us. There was no time to do anything other than to blast the horn and fortunately, the children saw us in time and scrambled clear.

Approaching Romford, speed was climbing again with a great deal of engine noise. We passed Romford station on the 'up' main at 14.20 and at a full 60 mph. As we roared through the station I noticed Class 315 emu No.315802 on the branch shuttle to Upminster. The platforms were crowded with passengers as we passed and a number took a step back as No.47590 roared through with its 25 wagons. Approaching Whale Bone Lane bridge we noticed that the next signal was showing a single amber aspect. Dave began to apply the brakes gently in case we had to stop. It was newer ballast at this location and I noticed that the ride had become much harder in the cab. We passed Chadwell Heath signal box intact but not functioning. As we approached the weed infested remains of Goodmayes Yard the feather was 'off' for us to enter the passing loop. Dave said that this was undoubtedly to enable another 'up'

Our guard, Mr Trimingham, and a trainee guard prepare to look over the train before climbing into the rear cab of Class 47 No.47590 *Thomas Telford*. They only travelled as far as Stratford station, this being a driver-only job from that point.

Michael J. Collins

An opportunity to descend from the footplate of Class 47 No.47590 *Thomas Telford* when it was halted at signals at the top of Brentwood Bank during the run described in the text.
Michael J. Collins.

Just before we had to call the police because we were being vandalised! Class 47 No.47590 halted by signals in Goodmayes Loop as Class 86/2 No.86226 *Royal Mail Midlands* sweeps by with a Norwich-Liverpool Street express.
Michael J. Collins

Norwich express to pass us. As we passed slowly along the loop I looked at the junk-strewn remains of the yard. Bob must have been thinking similar thoughts to me and he recalled the heyday of steam when this location boasted a turntable and even a hump yard for shunting. We reminisced about the procession of steam hauled freights which must have passed here. As Class 86 No.86226 swept past us on the 13.00 Norwich-Liverpool Street things began to liven up. We were actually being attacked by vandals! They had crept out from behind bushes in the weed-strewn yard and began interfering with containers at the rear of the train. Bob and I decided to give chase but they disappeared and Bob reported the incident to the signalman who called the police. We heard the nearby neighbourhood erupt with the raucous sound of police car sirens and in about five minutes a police 'Panda' car appeared from behind the bushes near the station. The police chased off in the direc-

tion of our criminals but to no avail; after a few minutes they came back empty handed. Meanwhile we had been over to Goodmayes box for a chat with the signalman. Neither Dave nor Bob had visited this box since the days of steam so it was an interesting diversion for all concerned!

When we returned to the locomotive we climbed aboard and the cab began to get crowded because three police officers did the same thing – Metropolitan Police Officers don't often get the chance of a footplate ride either! After getting the road we slowly pulled away and paused for a moment at Goodmayes station for our police visitors to disembark. Soon we roared off onto the main line with 6,000 amps showing on the dial.

In a matter of moments we were passing Seven Kings station and within seconds we noticed Ilford car sheds on our right with dozens of stabled emus waiting to be called to action in the afternoon peak. I noticed a number of Class

315s in Network SouthEast livery, together with No.308138 still in blue and grey livery. We passed Ilford station at 15.42 at a steady 42 mph. Beyond the station we passed under the flyover to remain on the 'up' fast line. Approaching Forest Gate station a Class 86 flashed past us hauling the 15.05 Liverpool Street-Harwich boat train. Then another red light at signal F22. Bob climbed down to telephone up to enquire about the problem. There had been a track circuit failure and we were given permission to pass at danger. At this point we passed "Crompton" Class 33 No.33013 working a train of dead emus from Ilford depot which, doubtless, it was taking to Eastleigh Works for overhaul. Class 33s are not a common sight on the GE main line. At Forest Gate Junction we passed Class 37 No.37709 in its new oil sector Railfreight livery heading west with a train of tanks from Thameshaven. Passing Maryland station emu No.315813 passed with yet another commuter train from Liverpool Street – at this point there seemed to be trains coming from all directions. Shortly after we drew to a halt in Platform 9 at Stratford station and we said goodbye to our guard; this being a driver-only operated train from Stratford.

We paused at signal S31 and Bob and Dave climbed down to telephone the signalman. They wanted to contact Dalston Junction box to ensure that we were given the 'B' freight road across the North London Line. They were anxious that we went this way because there was a 10 mph speed restriction on the other track and No.47590 might stick with this heavy load on the heavily graded lines. This completed we received permission to proceed and Dave opened up the controller. The locomotive surged into life and 4,000 amps showed on the ammeter. Nothing happened. The engine note changed and 5,000 amps was showing. Nothing happened. With a surge of power the engine really started to rev up and we began to crawl forward at 2 mph with 6,000 amps showing just for a moment on the ammeter.

At Stratford Central Junction we passed one of the Yeoman Type 59s, No.59004 *Yeoman Challenger* bound for Purfleet with another load of stone. I noticed High Meeds curve on the right as we passed. This is the line which many enthusiasts know as the freight only line that passes immediately behind Stratford heavy repairs shops and gives access to Temple Mills Yard. This is the route taken also by Freightliner trains which have crossed London from the west and wish to enter the nearby Freightliner terminal. At the junction we picked up the tracks which are electrified at 750 volts dc for passage of the 2 EPB Southern electric units which at this time formed the Richmond-North Woolwich service. Since my trip, these local services have been diagrammed for Class 313 emus based at Bletchley depot. The line has also been electrified at 25kV ac in preparation for electric haulage of Freightliner trains such as this one which were going right through to Willesden. In fact these services went over to electric operation in the May following my cab trip. We crossed over the canal and Dave recounted the rather gory story of a girl's body which had been found in it recently. She had been murdered in a Richmond-North Woolwich train and dumped over the side as the train passed this spot. At 15.29 we were passing Hackney Wick station and as we approached we passed Class 37s Nos 37221 and 37140 heading towards Stratford with another Freightliner train. This line carries a heavy traffic in container trains heading for both Stratford and the East Coast ports as well as other freight and a twenty minute interval passenger emu service.

Soon we passed Homerton station at 29 mph and in another couple of minutes we approached Hackney Central. A group of blind people with white sticks were standing on the platform and Dave gave them a gentle warning on the horn just to make sure that they were aware of our approach. Here we passed underneath the Liverpool Street-Cambridge line and a Class 315 emu passed overhead forming a service to Hertford East. At Navarine Road Junction we remarked about the Graham Road Curve which was visible and allows through running on peak hour trains of Class 313 emus from Liverpool Street to Watford. We took the North London Line and all three of us breathed a sigh of relief when we realised that Dalston Junction box had done its work properly and we were given the 'B' road as requested. The railway is very enclosed along this stretch with high walled cuttings with houses on top. It was amazing what people had tipped down the cuttings – old push chairs, artificial legs, old baths, prams, general litter and muck were strewn all over tracks. It is a wonder that derailments seldom happen along this stretch with so much rubbish about.

At Canonbury Junction the double freight lines along which we were travelling were reduced to single track. This was done to allow the economical erection of overhead wires through some of the bridges which are rather tight for clearance in these parts. We passed the warning board for the 10 mph speed restrictions which applied to the dc lines only. We proceeded at a steady 30 mph or so. Dave remarked that it was a good bet that had we been routed on to the dc line we would have stalled to a stand whilst accelerating away from this slack with such a heavy load. Soon we passed Canonbury Junction with the line to the Great Northern system at Finsbury Park curving away to our right through a tunnel. At Highbury station we passed yet another Richmond to Woolwich service with 2-EPB unit No.6322 forming the traction. We all remarked at its graffiti covered front end which looked a real mess. In fact graffiti was everywhere on this stretch of railway – on walls, footbridges, stations, posters and anywhere fairly accessible to anyone with a can of spray paint. It is costing BR thousands of pounds a week to clear up the mess and we all concurred when Bob remarked that it was the social disease of the century.

Soon we approached Caledonian Road station and we picked up double track again. On the approach to the station we passed the site of one of the original Freightliner depots at Maiden Lane. Fairly inevitably it has, since closure, been razed to the ground and converted into a housing estate. After passing the station we crossed high above the King's Cross main line and we could see the site of the former steam shed and King's Cross goods yard far below us. Curiously there was another Freightliner depot in this yard but this was closed down during economic cuts in the mid-1980s. At Camden Road we left the freight line and joined the 750 volt dc tracks. This is because we were about to fork left at Camden Road Junction to take the short line which leads down through Primrose Hill and to the WCML. This stretch of line was electrified at 25kV ac at the same time as the west coast route itself so that electrically hauled freights could reach the North London line before needing to change over traction to diesel haulage. Curiously it has hardly ever been used – at least in recent times – but it will now claim a new lease of life with overhead electrification of the North London lines.

Again we crossed a canal and we noticed the hundreds of boats tied up at the moorings and we passed the old steam roundhouse at Camden – still extant but now used as a theatre. We joined the WCML and the feather was 'off'

Shot from the cab window of Class 47 No.47590 as we approached Hackney Wick on the North London Line. Two unidentified Class 37s pass us heading east with the 06.22 Holyhead-Stratford Freightliner.
Michael J. Collins

No. 47590 halted at signals again on the WCML at Kilburn Loop. The main west coast route can be seen on the right and part of the London Transport underground train maintenance facility at Queen's Park on the left.
Michael J. Collins

at Primrose Hill Tunnel and Dave gave a long blast as we entered the tunnel. This is a very long bore and the headlight on No.47590 illuminated our passage through the gloomy depths. Way ahead I could see a tiny gleam of light that marked daylight at the end of the tunnel. It was uphill all the way here, and I could hear the engine throbbing away behind us with the noise appearing to be all the louder as it echoed on the tunnel walls. The ammeter showed 4,000 amps all the way through the tunnel indicating that the locomotive was being worked quite hard. We plunged out into daylight at 15.46 and passed South Hampstead station. We received an amber signal at colour light WN 219 and Dave said that he had an idea that we were going to be looped at Kilburn. We slowly approached signal WN 79 which was glowing red and Dave braked heavily. We drew to a halt just yards from the signal. Dave jumped

down from the cab to catch a word with the signalman as a Class 313 unit clattered past us on a Euston-Watford working. Dave soon reappeared a little bit bemused. The signalman had stopped us because he was not sure what our train was! Anyway, we were definitely going to be held for a while in Kilburn loops. Dave accelerated our train slowly away as a Class 317 emu scuttled past us on a working to Milton Keynes.

We drew to a stand again at signal WN 179 at 15.53. We should have arrived at Willesden at 15.50. So, after all our problems we were still making good time and were only a little bit down on schedule. We waited for the signals and at this point Inspector Clow could resist the temptation no longer! He took the controls in order to give Dave a break and also to keep his own expert hand in. After a minute the light turned amber and Bob eased on the power. With

4,000 amps showing No.47590 roared into life and our long train was slowly on the move again. We passed into Kilburn a minute later. As we stopped, Class 85 No.85005 passed us heading south with empty Network SouthEast carriage stock from Wembley sidings to Euston which would form a commuter train to Northampton a little later in the day. As we paused in the loop Dave came a little more talkative as he was relieved from the concentration of driving. He told me that he is in Link 'B' at Stratford and that he drives diesels on passenger and freight as well as emus on passenger trains. His work takes him regularly to Whitemoor, Cambridge, Harwich Parkeston Quay and Ipswich. He also knows the route through to the Southern at Hither Green.

At 16.10 we received permission to leave the loop. We wound our way over a succession of crossovers to join the main line. I watched Bob lean his head out of the window to do the customary safety check of ensuring that our train was following on. As we passed through Queens Park station I noticed a London Transport underground train picking up another load of passengers destined for central London. Bob wound on the power as we climbed our way up the steep bank beyond the station. Class 87 No.87002 passed, heading south with a Glasgow-Euston express. Shortly afterwards we passed Willesden Traction Maintenance Depot. It was a weekday so most of the allocation was out on the line working, but on depot today I noticed a stranger in the form of Class 47 No.47152 together with electric locomotives Nos 83015 and 82006 stabled outside.

Approaching the bridge which takes the North London line over the WCML we passed onto the 'down' goods line preparatory to entering the Freightliner terminal. Again we had a red light and we drew to a stand at signal WN 117.

After just a short pause the feather went off and we noticed that the points ahead were set and Bob applied power. With 2,500 amps showing on the dial we drew forward slowly. I noticed Class 08 No.08905 standing as we entered the Freightliner terminal. Dave leaned right out of the driver's side window as we passed one of the workers at the terminal and handed him our papers which detailed the load and destination of each wagon. The shunter climbed aboard ready to indicate where to stop at the appropriate time. Bob slowed down to less than walking pace and the shunter jumped down and ran ahead. Bob watched his hand signals keenly and at exactly the right spot he indicated to stop. In seconds our train had been uncoupled from the locomotive. Bob drew forward and Dave took the controls again. We were due for a leisurely drive light engine across the North London Lines and back to Stratford depot. This was the end of Dave's turn and after disposing of the locomotive we alighted and he bade us farewell. For the two BR men it was just another humdrum day of work. They could not understand what it was that I was getting excited about! Now I can tell them. For me it was a fascinating day. It was a day which gave me a unique insight into the operations of Freightliner trains. A day full of interest and I would like to thank them both for their kindness in sharing their working day with me. I also thank them for putting up with my fool questions! They were both patience personified.

Another shot from the cab of Class 47 No.47590 on the run described in the text as the train arrives at Willesden Freightliner Terminal. Older readers will remember the giant steam locomotive depot which used to occupy this site.

Michael J. Collins

Birmingham Bound

Approaching Ryecroft Junction, north of Walsall, on 16th June 1984 is Class 31 No.31282 with the 11.05 Leeds-Lawley Street Freightliner. In the background can be seen the now closed Walsall-Lichfield freight only line. *Geoff Dowling*

Class 58s are a welcome but increasingly rare sight on Freightliners. Bathed in early autumn sunshine No.58030 passes Tyseley, in the Birmingham suburbs, with the 12.35 Southampton Maritime-Lawley Street service of 20th September 1986. *Geoff Dowling*

As it reverses the 18.45 service to Glasgow out of the Freightliner terminal Class 56 No.56108 propels some of its load into Dudley Tunnel. The bracket signal in front of the locomotive indicates that the train already has permission to proceed.

Geoff Dowling

Business seems slack on the 09.25 Lawley Street-Southampton Millbrook service on 25th February 1984 as it has only loaded to a 5-set of wagons. Now withdrawn Class 33 No.33005 passes Hatton station Junction on this dull late winter day.

Geoff Dowling

Booked for Class 50 haulage for some months during 1983 was the 20.20 service from Lawley Street-Felixstowe. Passing Bromford Bridge is No.50016 *Barham* on this working on 5th May 1983. The diesel would have been removed in favour of electric traction at Nuneaton.

Geoff Dowling

Class 47 No.47041 is seen traversing the freight only Ryecroft Junction to Water Orton West Junction line on 16th May 1984. The train is the 05.42 Holyhead to Lawley Street service.

John Tuffs

This Saturday afternoon Freightliner from South Wales to Lawley Street made an uncommon sight as it approached Five Ways station in Birmingham because shortly it would be passing through New Street station where any freight is unusual. Class 45 No.45006 provides the power for the very lightly loaded train.

Michael J. Collins

Chapter 7

Freightliner Wagons

by Roger Silsbury

The prototype four-wagon set of container flats for the proposed liner train service was ordered from Shildon Works under Lot 3480 and was completed during January 1964. The design was of a skeletal framework carried on Davis & Lloyd Ridemaster, 6 ft 6¾ in wheelbase bogies fitted with 2 ft 8 in diameter wheels and roller bearing axleboxes, which gave a platform height of 3 ft 1 in above rail level. Braking was by means of automatic air brakes, with hand brakes for parking. Within the set there was no buffing gear, coupling being by fixed-head buckeye couplings which also acted as buffers, whilst at the outer ends the platform was extended and raised to accommodate oval headed, self contained buffers and drop-head buckeye couplings. The usable length of the wagons was 42 ft 6 in, the outer wagons being 45 ft 9 in long and the set being 179 ft 2 in, long overall. Four sets of container locating spigots were positioned at 10 ft 5¾ in centres and a mechanical container securing device was operated from the headstocks within the set; the original designed load was 30 tons but this was uprated to 40 tons before delivery. These wagons and the prototype containers detailed in the next chapter were exhibited at Marylebone during March 1964 before touring the country for display to prospective customers.

The principle having been established, production sets of Freightliner wagons, (the name Freightliner having been selected as the marketing brandname), were ordered from Ashford Works and apart from 155 vehicles built at Shildon during 1967 when demand outstripped capacity at Ashford, all construction of Freightliner flats was at the Kent works. The production vehicles differed from the prototypes; the basic skeletal structure was increased in length to a 62 ft 6 in platform with outer vehicles having a one foot extension to accommodate the buffing gear. A special design of Oleo pneumatic buffer with 1 ft 10 in round heads and 1 ft 10 in projection was fitted and this type of buffer has remained peculiar to Freightliner flats. A conventional screw coupling hook was fitted to the outer ends,

but no coupling was originally fitted, it being necessary to use the locomotive coupling to attach to the train. Within the set a specially designed rigid bar coupler was fitted which also carried the air brake pipe connections, four bolts and nuts being needed to hold pairs of couplers together.

The design load was 51 tons, which has subsequently been uprated to 62 tonnes for the majority of vehicles. The initial order for 100 vehicles (18 outer and 82 inner) was planned to be run in fixed formations of 15 wagon sets, although this could be varied according to experience. Container locating pins were at the standard 10 ft 5¾ in centres and a system of air-operated container clamps replaced the mechanical system of the prototype. Bogies were 6 ft 6¾ in (2 metre) wheelbase Ridemaster, with wheel-mounted disc brakes and these initial vehicles became known as Batch I, being painted in black livery. Quite soon after delivery twelve inner wagons were modified by the fitting of brackets to enable ISO containers to be carried and this modification was eventually made to all vehicles. The next 890 wagons delivered (318 Outer and 572 Inner) were fitted with ISO locating devices from new and were known as Batch II vehicles. A new type of bogie, known as Ride control BR 2M and featuring axle-mounted Girling disc brakes was fitted, Mark I to outer vehicles and Mark II to inners, and they were painted in blue livery to provide a visual indication of the differences from the Batch I type. Apart from the first one hundred, an electric warning lamp, positioned on the headstock, was incorporated into the Freightliner container clamping circuit and this was retrospectively fitted to the other existing wagons. Also during this period a single experimental wagon was produced which had conventional buffing and drawgear at both ends.

By 1968 it was accepted that the purely Freightliner system of container location and lifting would have to give way to the ISO system and vehicles built from Lot 3675 onwards dispensed with the air-operated Freightliner container clamping system, although provision existed for the

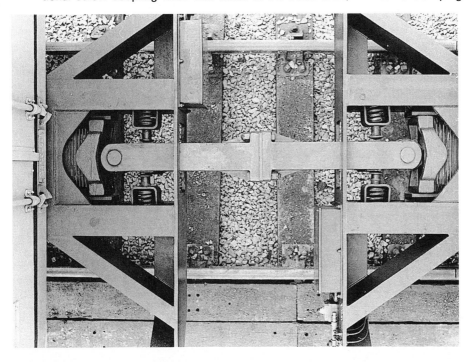

Close up of the unique rigid bar coupler used for Freightliner wagons within each set.
Michael J. Collins

carriage of the older style containers using hand clamps. A year later, with Lot 3711, the Freightliner system was abandoned for new buildings. These later vehicles have not carried any designation, although they could logically be considered Batch III. Two types of bogie were fitted to vehicles built under Lots between 3654 and 3712, the Ride control BR 2M Marks I and II and Freightliner F/L 1, thereafter production was standardised on the Mark III version of the BR 2M which reverted to wheel-mounted disc pads.

The accompanying *Table 3* gives full details of the various Freightliner flats built and some expansion on the Notes is necessary. Where the original Lot files indicated either the traffic or operator for which the relevant vehicles were being built, this has been noted. The note regarding fitments indicates that all subsequent vehicles were so equipped. The final three lots listed cover rebuildings: Lot 3924 was for two inner wagons, 602206 and 602331, which were given conventional buffing and drawgear at both ends in the same manner as B601999 and were intended for service to the Far North of Scotland, being equipped with vacuum through pipes to enable them to run in passenger train formations. Initially coded FGB they were subsequently

recorded FJB to differentiate them from the single ended outer wagons. No. 601996 had also started life as an inner wagon, No. RDB602548 allocated to the Research Department at Derby. In 1976 it was converted to double ended configuration, still with the Research Department, but in 1980 was released to general traffic with the other double ended vehicles. Lot 3964 was issued for the conversion of 24 inner wagons to outers, all donor vehicles being drawn from Lot 3499; experience had shown that even the five-vehicle rakes which had by then become the standard formation were occasionally too large for some traffics and the addition of extra outer wagons would enable two and three vehicle sets to be run.

Freightliner flats were ideally suited for use as commercial vehicle carriers, because of their low platform height. Initially a demountable deck with angled end ramps which located on, and fixed to, the container securing pins was used, but eventually 15 vehicles became permanent vehicle carriers being fitted with fixed end ramps and wooden decks. Although no longer part of the Freightliner fleet these 15 (four outers, six inners converted to outers and five inners) retained their original numbers.

Renumberings

In readiness for the through Stratford-Paris service via the Dover-Dunkerque train ferry 21 outer and 14 inner wagons were given ferry fittings and renumbered into the international series early in 1968, becoming Nos 21 70 4384 000 – 020 and 21 70 4384 500 – 513 respectively. Later in 1968 Intercontainer, the European railway container consortium, leased a batch of 28 outer and 36 inner wagons. These were also given ferry fittings and renumbered; initially the exchange condition number was to be 21, but this was amended to 20, the full numbers being 20 70 0499 000 – 027 (outers) and 20 70 0499 500 – 535 (inners). Upon the cessation of these international services the wagons were released into normal traffic without modification and as sets were split during overhaul, they gradually became dispersed. Although orders were issued to renumber them back to their original domestic numbers, this was not reported as done until 1980!

This ground level photograph gives a good view of the early Davis & Lloyd Ridemaster bogies as fitted to Freightliner flats. Wagon No.B601003 in the foreground was built at Ashford in 1964 under Lot No.3498 and is one of the initial 100 vehicles which comprised Batch I.

One of the early Batch II Freightliner flats No.B601161 at an exhibition of rolling stock at Waterloo on 23rd June 1967.
John Scrace

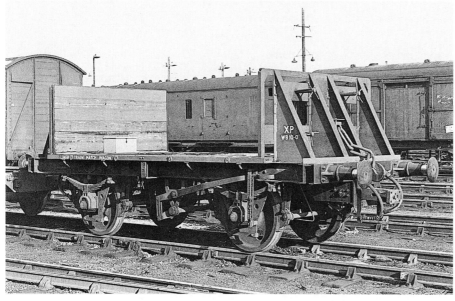

A liner train match wagon at Old Oak Common on 7th April 1963.The bar coupling can be seen between the buffers in addition to the normal wagon coupling equipment.

Alec Swain

Most Freightliner trains have balancing workings so it is unusual to see completely empty container sets out on the main line. This set, headed by Class 47 No.47298 as it passed Twyford on 23rd April 1983, was being taken to Stratford for repair.

Michael J. Collins

In February 1980 it was decided to renumber certain vehicles in order that they should be readily identifiable to the TOPS computer. The 85 remaining Batch I wagons were to have their numbers increased by 10,000, the 28 outers becoming 611XXX series and 57 inners 612XXX series. Two hundred and sixteen vehicles with F/L 1 bogies were to have their numbers increased by 20,000, although ultimately a total of 243 wagons (95 outers and 138 inners) were identified, becoming 621XXX and 622XXX series respectively. By the end of 1989 all the Batch I wagons had been withdrawn with the exception of two outers

involved in Minilink trials and all F/L 1 bogie fitted wagons either withdrawn or transferred to rubbish train use and recoded FYA (outer) or FUA (inner).

Other wagons

In 1966 three 25 Ton, 2-axle container wagons were built at Ashford using the prototype BR standard wagon underframe then under development. This gave a 31 ft 6 in clear platform, the 2 ft 8 in diameter wheels permitting a 3 ft $3\frac{1}{4}$ in high deck. A year later, Shildon Works produced a

This rearward view of the 12.20 Lawley Street-Southampton Maritime service gives an impression of the weight-saving skeletal structure of Freightliner wagons. The train is seen passing Aynho Junction on 17th September 1988 behind Class 47 No.47008.
Michael J. Collins

further 20, the entire batch being allocated to Irish Shipping services. Both Freightliner and ISO locating points were provided. By 1972 they had passed out of this traffic and were spread amongst various domestic services. Also in 1966 the Freightliner concept had generated traffics which could not be adequately served by full Freightliner services and 100 Lowmac wagons, basically all to the same design, received frameworks fitted into the well to enable them to carry one 20 ft ISO container on ordinary freight services. Expansion of the Freightliner network rendered these converted Lowmacs redundant by 1972, and they passed out of container traffic.

At the beginning of the 1970s both the CM&EE and the CCE were expressing dissatisfaction with the bogie behaviour and running costs of the existing Freightliner fleet. As designed, the original vehicles were built for 8 ft x 8 ft containers and were limited to 51 ton load. The potential ability to carry 60 tons (three TEU's, ie three 20 ft, or one 20 ft and one 40 ft boxes), coupled with the increasing preponderance of 40 ft long containers in the Deep Sea trade led to three prototype wagon sets being developed. The first was not exclusively for containers; it consisted of a five wagon set of 2-axle vehicles, 2 ft 6 in diameter wheels permitting a floor height of only 2 ft 10½ in. ISO twistlocks for container stowage and detachable vehicle ramps on the outer wagons, with hinged bridging plates between vehicles within the set, permitted either containers or commercial vehicles to be carried, although the low carrying capacity of only 10 tons per vehicle biased them

towards the latter and it is in this traffic that they quickly settled. The other two sets were exclusively container wagons, however. Both were two-vehicle, bogie sets, the 'body' consisting of nothing more than winged plates to accommodate the container securing devices extending sideways from the two main longitudinals of the underframe. Conventional buffing and drawgear was fitted at the outer ends only, a bar coupler being used between. Location points for both ISO and Sealand containers was provided, these being the only wagons on BR to provide the Sealand fitting. It is worth mentioning here that Sealand is an American company which in the late 1960s was endeavouring to impose its own container standards internationally, but which were rejected in favour of the ISO standards. The difference in the two sets was that Lot 3729 comprised wagons 42 ft long carried on four-wheeled bogies and was designated 'Lowliner A' whilst those to Lot 3730 were 62 ft long and had six-wheeled bogies and was 'Lowliner B'; both used wheels of only 2 ft 4 in diameter giving a floor height of 2 ft 10 in. These sets were never developed into series production.

Two further experimental vehicles have been built, both in 1981. Intriguingly, the BR vehicle, No. RDB998546 for the

Freightliner flats do have to go for works repair occasionally. This photograph was taken during January 1988 at Wolverton Works which had the contract to do a number of major repairs at this time.
Michael J. Collins

Research Department, came from private builder, Standard Wagon, whilst BREL Shildon produced No. F93000 as a privately registered vehicle. Neither vehicle has progressed beyond the experimental stage. *Table 3* lists those non-standard vehicles.

When Freightliner trains first began running accommodation had to be provided for the guard. Initially a small number of container type 'caboose' were provided, but these were extremely unpopular and in response to union demands a series of redundant coaches were adapted for use as Freightliner train brake vans. The details are contained in *Table 5* and they remained in service until union agreement was negotiated for the guard to ride in the rear cab of the locomotive.

Finally, mention must be made of a series of Freightliner adaptor wagons. Because of the unique coupling arrangements within Freightliner sets, special adaptor wagons fitted with compatible couplers were needed when sets were disbanded for works attention, 54 redundant Palbrick B wagons from Lot 3254 being converted for this use.

Table 3 **Freightliner Wagons – Details**

Lot	Number series	Total	Builder	Date	Diag	Length	D.Code	Bogie	Notes
Pt.3480	B601001-B601002	2	Shildon	01/64	080	45′ 9″	FG002A	SH	Ordered 30T, delivered 40T load.
Pt.3480	B602001-B602002	2	Shildon	01/64	081	42′ 6″	FF002A	SH	
3498	B601003-B601020	18	Ashford	11/64-10/65	082	63′ 6″	FG004A	SH	Batch I
3499	B602003-B602084	82	Ashford	06/64-04/66	083	62′ 6″	FF001A	SH	Batch I
3559	B601021-B601061	41	Ashford	08/66-01/67	084	63′ 6″	FG004G	SJ	Batch II
3560	B602085-B602143	59	Ashford	09/66-01/67	086	62′ 6″	FF001B	SK	Batch II
3585	B601999	1	Ashford	10/66	122	64′ 6″	FG004F	SJ	Experimental. AOC/el.h/s
3596	B601062-B601091	30	Ashford	11/66-12/66	084	63′ 6″	FG004C	SJ	Batch II AOC/el.h/s. Irish, AB & VP
3602	B601092-B601147	56	Ashford	01/67-03/67	084	63′ 6″	FG004G	SJ	Batch II P.Quay
3618	B602144-B602220	77	Ashford	03/67-07/67	086	62′ 6″	FF001B	SK	Batch II 71 Ftlr, 6 TA.
3619	B601148-B601175	28	Ashford	03/67-07/67	084	63′ 6″	FG004G	SJ	Batch II 24 Ftlr, 4 TA.
3621	B602221-B602296	76	Shildon	06/67-09/67	086	62′ 6″	FF001B	SK	Batch II 22 Ftlr, 54 TDG.
3622	B601176-B601204	29	Shildon	06/67-10/67	084	63′ 6″	FG004G	SJ	Batch II 17 Ftlr, 12 TDG.
3626	B602297-B602386	90	Ashford	08/67-10/67	086	62′ 6″	FF001B	SK	Batch II

Lot	Number series	Total	Builder	Date	Diag	Length	D.Code	Bogie	Notes
3627	B601205-B601240	36	Ashford	08/67-10/67	084	63′ 6″	FG004G	SJ	Batch II
3638	B602387	1	Ashford	12/67	086	62′ 6″	FF001B	SK	Batch II TA.
3639	B601241-B601245	5	Ashford	12/67	084	63′ 6″	FG004G	SK	Batch II TA.
3652	B602388-B602721	334	Ashford	10/67-11/69	086	62′ 6″	FF001B/E	SK	Batch II (to 602614 + 602718/721)
3653	B602772-B602811	40	Shildon	11/67-12/67	086	62′ 6″	FF001B	SK	Batch II
Pt.3654	B601246-B601335	90	Ashford	10/67-06/68	084	63′ 6″	FG004B	SK	Batch II (to 601328)
Pt.3654	B601346-B601395	50	Ashford	06/68-11/68	084	63′ 6″	FG004B	SK	
3655	B601336-B601345	10	Shildon	11/67-12/67	084	63′ 6″	FG004B	SK	Batch II
3675	B601396-B601444	49	Ashford	10/68-02/69	123	63′ 6″	FG004D	SK	No AOC
Pt.3676	B602722-B602771	50	Ashford	10/68-02/69	124	62′ 6″	FF001C	SM	
Pt.3676	B602812-602911	100	Ashford	12/68-05/69	124	62′ 6″	FF001E	SK	
3689	B602912-B602947	36	Ashford	05/69-10/69	124	62′ 6″	FF001C	SM	lc.
3690	B601445-B601468	24	Ashford	02/69-04/69	123	63′ 6″	FG004D	SK	lc.
3691	B602948-B602951	4	Ashford	09/69	124	62′ 6″	FF001C	SM	Irish
3692	B601469-B601493	25	Ashford	04/69-11/69	123	63′ 6″	FG004D	SK	Irish
3711	601494-601527	34	Ashford	10/69-04/70	123	63′ 6″	FG004D	SK	ISO only
3712	602952-603029	78	Ashford	10/69-05/70	124	62′ 6″	FF001C	SM	
3718	601528-601603	76	Ashford	12/70-06/71	125	63′ 6″	FG004E	SL	Irish
3741	601604-601629	26	Ashford	01/71-07/71	126	63′ 6″	FG004E	SL	2 TA, 24 Ftlr. M/T assem.
3742	603030-603075	46	Ashford	12/70-07/71	126	62′ 6″	FF001D	SL	10 TA, 36 Ftlr.
3765	601630-601653	24	Ashford	07/71-11/71	125	63′ 6″	FG004E	SL	OCL/ACT Fareast trade, lease H.S.
3766	603076-603111	35	Ashford	07/71-11/71	126	62′ 6″	FF001D	SL	OCL/ACT Fareast trade, lease H.S.
3767	601654-601689	36	Ashford	01/72-08/72	125	63′ 6″	FG004E	SL	OCL/ACT Fareast trade.
3768	603112-603163	52	Ashford	01/72-08/72	126	62′ 6″	FF001D	SL	OCL/ACT Fareast trade.
3806	603164-603250	87	Ashford	02/73-09/73	126	62′ 6″	FF001D	SL	
3807	601690-601762	72	Ashford	02/73-10/73	125	63′ 6″	FG004E	SL	
3847	601763-601849	87	Ashford	12/74-11/76	125	63′ 6″	FG004E	SL	TOPS coded from new
3848	603251-603274	24	Ashford	12/74-06/75	126	62′ 6″	FF001D	SL	
3924	601997-601998	2	T.Mills	?/77	–	64′ 6″	FG008A	SK	
3964	601850-601863	24	Horwich	07/79-12/79	–	63′ 6″	FG004K	SH	
3980	RDB601996	1	T.Mills	03/80	–	64′ 6″	FJ001A	SK	

Bogie types.

SH	=	Ride master
SJ	=	Ride control BR 2M MkI
SK	=	Ride control BR 2M MkII
SL	=	Ride control BR 2M MkIII
SM	=	F/L 1

Key to Notes regarding fittings and operators.

AOC/el.h/s	=	Air operated container clamps, electric light indicator on headstock
No AOC	=	No air operated clamps fitted.
M/T assem.	=	Multilock Twistlock assembly.
Irish	=	For Irish Shipping services.
P.Quay.	=	For Parkeston Quay services.
Ftlr.	=	Freightliner services.
lc.	=	Leased to Intercontainer.
TA	=	Tartan Arrow services.
TDG	=	Transport Development group services.
lease H.S.	=	Leased to Hill, Samuel.

Notes regarding amendments to Lots.

Lot 3618 – Originally for 153 vehicles, numbered B602144-B602220; balance to lot 3621.

Lot 3619 – Originally for 57 vehicles, numbered B601148-B601204; balance to lot 3622.

Lot 3652 – Originally for 384 vehicles, numbered B602388-B602771; balance of Batch III vehicles added to Lot 3676.

Lot 3675 – Originally for 99 vehicles, 50 diverted to Inners under lot 3676.

Lot 3676 – Originally for 100 vehicles, 50 ex-lot 3652 plus 50 new; increased by diversion of 50 outers from lot 3675 to inners.

Lot 3741 – Originally for two vehicles, increased to 26.

Lot 3742 – Originally for ten vehicles, increased to 46.

Table 4 Other Container Wagons

Lot	Number series	Total	Builder	Date	Diag	Length	D.Code	Brake
3566	B511000-511002	3	Ashford	04/66-05/66	074	33′ 6″	FB001A	AB&AVB
3620	B511003-511022	20	Shildon	08/67-09/67	079	33′ 6″	FB001A	AB&VP
3713	150000-150001	2	Ashford	07/70	127	41′ 6″	FZ005A	AB. Dual container/vehicle wagons.
3714	150002-150004	3	Ashford	07/70	128	40′ 0″	FZ004A.	Dual container/vehicle wagons.
3729	699000-699001	2	Ashford	09/71	135	42′ 0″	FG003A	AB Disc
3730	699002-699003	2	Ashford	12/71-01/72	136	62′ 0″	FG005A	AB Disc
–	22/25T Lowmacs	100		1966 +	059	30′ 0″	FS001	AVB
–	RDB998546	1	Standard	–/81	–		YX039A	Test vehicle
–	F93000	1	Shildon	–/81	–		PF006A	Experimental wagon

Table 5 Freightliner Brake Vans, Ex-Coaching Stock
Conversion details

Lot	Vehicle No.	Orig. No.	Type	Built	Conv. at	Date	Lot	Vehicle No.	Orig. No.	Type	Built	Conv. at	Date
3598	DB963901	M30820M	BG	1929	Gushetfaulds	06/66		DB963933	M30427M	BG	1925	Swindon	07/67
	DB963902	M30926M	BG	1933	Gushetfaulds	06/66		DB963934	Sc43311	BS	1955	Swindon	07/67
	DB963903	M30962M	BG	1934	Gushetfaulds	06/66		DB963935	Sc43313	BS	1955	Swindon	07/67
	DB963904	S43383	BS	1956	Garston	06/66 +		DB963936	Sc43201	BS	1954	Swindon	07/67
	DB963905	S4251S	BSK	1948	Garston	06/66		DB963937	Sc43340	BS	1955	Swindon	07/67
	DB963906	S43382	BS	1956	Garston	08/66		DB963938	Sc43315	BS	1955	Swindon	07/67
	DB963907	M31065M	BG	1939	Longsight	07/66		DB963939	Sc43227	BS	1954	Swindon	07/67
	DB963908	E43136	BS	1955	Derby	07/66		DB963940	Sc43199	BS	1955	Swindon	07/67
	DB963909	E43155	BS	1955	Derby	07/66		DB963941	Sc43330	BS	1955	Swindon	07/67
	DB963910	E43119	BS	1955	Derby	07/66		DB963942	Sc43331	BS	1955	Swindon	07/67
	DB963911	M43277	BS	1955	Derby	08/66		DB963943	Sc43215	BS	1954	Swindon	08/67
	DB963912	M30591M	BG	1927	Derby	08/66		DB963944	Sc43332	BS	1955	Swindon	08/67
	DB963913	M43247	BS	1954	Derby	08/66		DB963945	Sc43202	BS	1954	Swindon	08/67
	DB963914	M43283	BS	1955	Derby	09/66		DB963946	Sc43212	BS	1954	Swindon	08/67
	DB963915	M26304M	BSK	1939	Derby	10/66		DB963947	Sc43314	BS	1955	Swindon	09/67 +
	DB963916	E26579M	BSK	1948	Derby	10/66		DB963948	Sc43218	BS	1954	Swindon	09/67
3614	DB963917	E43194	BS	1954	Derby	11/66		DB963949	Sc43200	BS	1954	Swindon	09/67
	DB963918	M21036M	BS	1949	Derby	11/66		DB963950	Sc43322	BS	1955	Swindon	09/67
	DB963919	M43257	BS	1954	Derby	11/66		DB963951	Sc43316	BS	1955	Swindon	09/67*
	DB963920	M26233M	BSK	1939	Derby	12/66		DB963952	Sc43326	BS	1955	Swindon	09/67*
	DB963921	M5722M	BSK	1935	Derby	01/67		DB963953	Sc43341	BS	1955	Swindon	09/67*
	DB963922	E26360M	BSK	1945	Derby	01/67		DB963954	Sc43335	BS	1955	Swindon	10/67
3643	DB963923	E43133	BS	1954	Swindon	03/67		DB963955	Sc43321	BS	1955	Swindon	10/67
	DB963924	E43114	BS	1954	Swindon	04/67		DB963956	Sc43337	BS	1955	Swindon	10/67
	DB963925	E43115	BS	1954	Swindon	04/67 +		DB963957	M30685M	BG	1928	Swindon	10/67
	DB963926	E43126	BS	1954	Swindon	06/67		DB963958	M30735M	BG	1928	Swindon	10/67
	DB963927	E43132	BS	1954	Swindon	06/67		DB963959	M30739M	BG	1928	Swindon	10/67
	DB963928	E43134	BS	1954	Swindon	06/67		DB963960	M26463M	BSK	1946	Swindon	11/67
	DB963929	E43135	BS	1954	Swindon	06/67							
	DB963930	E43139	BS	1954	Swindon	06/67							
	DB963931	E43144	BS	1954	Swindon	06/67	+	To crane runner					
	DB963932	Sc43342	BS	1955	Swindon	07/67	*	To BTU tool van					

Opposite page top: A view of Stratford Major Depot with Freightliner vehicles under repair. Also visible is Class 86 No.86255 *Penrith Beacon* together with Class 87 No.87032 *Kenilworth* and HST Power Car No.43084 *County of Derbyshire* which was in for conversion to a DVT.

Michael J. Collins

Left: During 1989 a number of container flats were hired from the wagon leasing firm of Tiphook for use on Freightliner services. One of these is seen at Leeds Terminal on 22nd August 1989.

Michael J. Collins

Chapter 8

Containers

by Roger Silsbury

Prior to the birth of the Liner Train concept there were two express container services available for general merchandise, both London Midland Region initiatives. The "Condor" service between London and Glasgow used existing RCH type containers, whilst the more wide ranging 'Speedfreight' system used a new breed of light metal containers requiring specially adapted Conflat wagons. Being modern containers, some of the Speedfreight types were subsequently modified for use by Freightliner.

To complement the prototype Liner Train wagons, a variety of prototype containers were ordered from both railway workshops and private builders. These comprised box, open and hooded types, BR lot numbers were issued for all these containers, all except one lot being for single examples, although only those built at railway workshops appear to have had drawn diagrams issued. Within given parameters, each design team was allowed a free hand and a variety of livery styles were applied to enable a corporate livery to be determined. Beside these general purposes types, three demonstrator tank containers were ordered during 1965, although it is unclear whether BR intended to offer series production or whether they were purely to persuade customers to build similar types of their own. Two sheeted tipping containers were also built during 1965 and used as demonstrators, but do not appear to have become part of the Freightliner fleet. Full details of all containers built for Freightliner, both when it was an integral part of the British Railways Board and since becoming an independent subsidiary, are given in the accompanying table.

Handling and securing

The original Freightliner concept used grappler arms from a frame spreader, the arms locating into pockets built into the base of the container. On rail, spigots on the wagon located into pockets in the load-bearing sub-frame base of the container, further movement being prevented by a

One of the 'Speedfreight' containers which were constructed of light alloy and fitted to specially adapted Conflat wagons.

The first Freightliner container No.001A. It is of 7.5 tons capacity, with steel frames and aluminium body and it is loaded on to one of the prototype wagons. It is seen at an exhibition of prototype Freightliner stock held at the Marylebone Goods Depot, London in March 1964 to which over 500 traders and road hauliers were invited.

Also on display at Marylebone in March 1964 was this 20 ft long monocoque construction 15 ton container. It was built using glass reinforced plastic technology at BR Eastleigh Works. Numbered 001B it was finished in a colour scheme of Bauxite, with yellow band and green ''flash''.

A covered container of 20 tons capacity on exhibition at Marylebone Goods Depot. It was constructed at BR Shildon Works with steel frames and aluminium body.

A prototype container designed for transit of bulk liquids such as beer or acids.

system of air-operated clamps which engaged into the sub-frame. The move to standard ISO fittings simplified handling and securing. Each container has ISO castings built into each top and bottom corner of the load-bearing frame, lifting being achieved by the spreader engaging into the top fittings, whilst locating/securing is by means of twistlocks engaging into the bottom fittings.

Numbering

The initial prototypes to Lots 3486-3490/3492 were originally issued with numbers following the Speedfreight containers, but these were amended to a totally new series before delivery, each type being given a number consisting of three digits, commencing 001, and an alpha suffix indicating type. The second batch of prototypes built under Lots 3501-3512 were issued with new series numbers from the beginning. One of the early decisions taken was to recognise the limitations of this new numbering system and the prototype containers were further renumbered into what became the standard Freightliner numbering form of two digits, one letter and two digits, the first two digits indicating a broad classification, the letter being container

A demonstration train of different containers ran on the ECML during the launch period of Freightliner to show potential customers what was available.

type and the final two digits, allied to the first two, giving individual identity. The most recent builds of container have been numbered into the accepted International series consisting of a four letter company identifier followed by a six figure individual identity.

Livery

Following assessment of the variety of liveries applied to the prototype containers a corporate livery of Rail Grey was decided upon. This was relieved by a 26in wide rail red horizontal band centred $31\frac{1}{2}$in above the base which, on open containers reached the top edge. The corporate 'double arrow' symbol appeared in white on the red band, longer boxes also carrying the 'Freightliner' name. the fleet numbers were red numerals and blue letter on a white patch, other lettering being black. This original livery was very smart and gave Freightliner trains a very uniform appearance. Minor variations gradually crept in, some open containers becoming overall red, and following the breakaway of Freightliner from the main BRB, the name when carried became 'Freightliners Limited'. In 1978 a new 'flagship' livery was introduced, consisting of the main body being painted blued-white with one end red, the red being carried around the sides and angled downwards at 45° and with a narrow red band paralleling the main red. The name 'Freightliner' was moved towards the top of the end away

from the red, it and other lettering being black. The lighter colour quickly dirtied, so in 1981 a simpler all-over red livery was adopted, relieved by a vertical white panel towards one end having the word 'Freightliner' in black vertically downwards above a small red triangle and line, other lettering becoming white. In 1983 the brand name was further modified to being written 'on end' from the bottom. The fusion of Freightliner and Speedlink into Railfreight Distribution has seen another new livery appear, with containers divided into red and yellow halves diagonally, yellow above, all lettering being black.

One of the earliest privately owned containers to run on Freightliner trains was of this type owned by the Cunard shipping company.

The first container behind the locomotive is interesting because it has an open top for conveying coal. It can also be placed on a tipper lorry if required. Class 45 No.45046 passes Gaer Junction, Newport, with a Freightliner from Swansea to Newcastle.
John Chalcraft

Class 37 No.37010 stands for a moment at Leeds while heading west with a Newcastle-Trafford Park Freightliner. Behind the locomotive is a container specially adapted for carrying bulk powders such as cement.

Michael J. Collins

A bulk malt container mounted on a road delivery vehicle painted in the 1960's livery, at Newcastle Terminal.

Early type Freightliner containers destined for Belfast being transferred from rail to ship at Heysham Harbour.

Table 6 Details of Freightliner Containers

Number series	Total	Builder	Year	BR Lot	BR Diag	Notes
Type A (1). 10′ Box, Non-ISO.						
00A01-00A02	2	Shildon	1964	3486	3/007	Orig. Nos 001A-002A
00A03-00A05	3	Derby	1964	3521	3/008	
00A06-00A33	28	Duralumin	1965	3538	3/008	
00A34-00A83	50	Horwich	1966	3593	3/008	
Type A (II). 40′ Box.						
10A01-10A12	12	Mod. Coat-bridge	1983			Length increased to 41′ 2″.
Type B (I). 20′ Box, Non-ISO.						
05B00	1	Eastleigh	1965	3490	3/033	Orig. No. 001B
05B01	1	Bonallack	1964	3501		Orig. No. 002B
05B02	1	GRC&W	1964	3502		Orig. No. 003B
05B03	1	J. Thompson	1964	3503		Orig. No. 004B
05B04	1	Duralumin	1964	3508		Orig. No. 005B
05B05	1	Derby	1964	3509	3/030	Orig. No. 006B
05B06-05B08	3	Derby	1964	3520	3/031	
05B09-05B14	6	Derby	1964	3529	3/031	
05B15-05B74	60	St Rollox	1965	3537	3/031	
05B75-06B24	50	St Rollox	1966	3594	3/031	

Number series	Total	Builder	Year	BR Lot	BR Diag	Notes
Type B (II). 20′ Pallet loading.						
94B00-94B08	9					
Type C (1). 27′ Box, Non-ISO.						
30C00	1	Shildon	1964	3488	3/180	Orig. No. 001C
30C01	1	Duralumin	1964	3504		Orig. No. 002C
30C02	1	York Trailer	1964	3510		Orig. No. 003C
30C03-30C05	3	Derby	1964	3522	3/181	
30C06-31C51	146	Derby	1965	3530	3/181	
Type C (II). 30′ Flat, 8′ 6″ wide.						
53C99-54C98	100	N.W. Trailer	1974			8′ 6″ wide
54C99-56C23	125	Moores	1983			8′ 6″ wide
90C75-92C20	126		1977/78			8′ 6″ wide: Modified from 54J99-56J98 series.
92C52-93C01	50		1978			8′ 6″ wide: Modified from 54J99-56J98 series.
93C02-93C21	20		1980			8′ 6″ wide: Modified from 68Y81-69Y80 series.
Type D (I). 30′ Box, Non-ISO.						
35D00-35D19	20	Derby	1966	3576	3/242	
35D20-35D69	50	Derby	1966	3595	3/065	
Type D (II). 40′ Boalloy Curtain-sided, 8′ 6″ high.						
20D00-20D01	2					
21D00-21D49	50	Adamson	1983			
21D50-21D93	44	Moores	1985			
Type F (I). 30′ Full side door, Non-ISO.						
62F50-62F54	5	Duralu- min/Derby	1966	3577	3/220	
Type F (II). 40′ Box, 8′ 6″ high.						
05F83-05F84	2					Purchased second-hand
05F85-06F24	40	W.H.Davis	1978/79			Purchased second-hand
06F25-06F74	50	Pacton	1974			
06F75-06F94	20	W.H.Davis	1978			
06F95-09F25	231	Jindo	1979			
09F26-09F80	55	Jindo	1980			
09F81-10F30	50	Jindo	1981			
10F31-10F80	50	Jindo	1982			
10F81-11F80	100	Various				Purchased second-hand 1982.
11F81-14F30	50	Jindo	1983			
14F31-18F30	400	Adamson	1985			
95F00-95F09	10	Jindo				Second-hand ex-Jindo fleet 1983/4.
95F50-95F51	2	Jindo	1983			Ex-12F36 & 12F41 for dedicated traffic
FLLU425001-425100	100	Adamson	1986			8′ 6″ high, 2.5m wide
FLLU425101-425200	100	Jindo	1987			8′ 6″ high, 2.5m wide
Type G. 10′ Box ISO (not so used).						
01G00-01G29	30	Cravens	1967	3605	3/080	
01G30-04G18	289	Horwich	1967	3628	3/081	
04G19-05G68	150	Derby	1968	3657	3/082	
Type H, 20′ Open, 1 fixed end, Non-ISO.						
25H00	1	Metro- Cammell	1964	3511		Orig. No. 001M
25H01	1	Metro- Cammell	1964	3512		Orig. No. 002M
25H02	1	Shildon	1964	3487	3/605	Orig. No. 001H
25H03	1	Metro- Cammell	1964	3505		
25H04	1	Derby	1964	3523		
25H05-25H08	4	St Rollox	1965	3545	3/607	
25H09-25H28	20	St Rollox	1965	3556	3/607	
25H29-25H54	26	Cowlairs	1966	3580	3/607	
25H55-25H84	30	Cowlairs	1966	3581	3/607	
25H85-26H29	45	Cowlairs	1966	3603	3/608	
26H30-26H49	20	Cowlairs	1967	3616	3/608	
26H50-28H08	159	St Rollox	1967	3631	3/632	
28H09-30H08	100	St Rollox	1968	3660	3/632	
30H09-32H08	200	St Rollox	1968	3681		

Number series	Total	Builder	Year	BR Lot	BR Diag	Notes
Type J (I), 27′ Open, 1 fixed end, Non-ISO.						
55J00	1	Shildon	1964	3489	3/625	Orig. No. 001J
55J01	1	Bonallack	1964	3506		Orig. No. 002J
55J02	1	Cravens	1964	3507	3/625	Orig. No. 003J
55J03	1	Derby	1964	3524	3/626	
55J04-55J11	8	St Rollox	1966	3546	3/627	
55J12-55J41	30	Cowlairs	1965	3557	3/627	
54J99 & 55J42-56J98	158	N.W.Trailers	1971/2			Converted 1977/8 & renumbered 90C75-93C01
Type J (II). 20′ Half height open.						
26J01-26J40	40	Various				Purchased second-hand 1981.
96J21-96J30	10					Dedicated traffic, ex-26J01-26J40 (range)
Type K. 30′ Open, 1 fixed end, Non-Iso.						
57K00-57K49	50	Cowlairs	1966	3582	3/615	
57K50-57K58	9	Cowlairs	1967	3617	3/645	
57K59-58K08	50	St Rollox	1967	3625	3/645	
58K09-61K28	320	St Rollox	1967	3632	3/646	
61K29	1	GRC&W	1967	3635		
61K30	1	GRC&W	1967	3662		
61K31-63K80	250	St Rollox	1968	3661	3/646	
63K81-68K80	500	St Rollox	1968	3664	3/646	
68K81-69K80	100	St Rollox	1969	3682		
Type L, 20′ Box.						
07L00-07L01	2	Thompson Trailer	1966	3600	3/191	
07L02-07L81	80	Cravens	1967	3606	3/194	
07L82-08L41	60	Thompson Trailer	1967	3607	3/192	
08L42-09L71	130	Horwich	1967	3610	3/193	
09L72	1	Watercraft	1967	3633		
09L73-14L63	491	Horwich	1968	3629	3/193	
14L64-17L13	250	Derby	1968	3656	3/195	
17L14-18L63	150	Derby	1968	3658		
18L64-20L63	200	Derby	1968	3672	3/195	
20L64-23L38	275	Derby	1968	3673		
23L39-24L38	100	Derby	1969	3693		
24L39-26L38	200	Derby	1969	3694		
26L39-27L38	100	Adamson	1972			
70L75-71L74	100	Adamson	1973			
71L75-72L74	50	York	1973			
72L75-72L74	50	Cravens	1973			
72L75-73L24	50	Adamson	1974			
75L51-78L50	300	Pacton	1974			8′ 6″ high
75L51-78L00	250	British Rail	1979			8′ 6″ high
81L01-83L77	277	Ulcon	1979			8′ 6″ high
83L78-83L85	8					8′ 6″ high
FLLU200001-200100	100	Evermaster	1986			8′ 6″ high, 2.5m wide
Type H. 30′ Curtain-sided.						
63M00-63M09	10					Boalloy
67M50	1	Derby	1965	3573	3/235	
65M51-67M56	6	Derby	1966	3604	2/235	
67M57-68M06	50	Derby	1967	3615	3/235	
68M07-69M06	100	Horwich	1968	3651	3/235	
69M07-69M81	75	Horwich	1968	3659	3/235	
74M00-74M15	16					Boalloy, M type reno. for dedicated traffic
83M00-84M13	114					Boalloy. M type reno. for dedicated traffic
85M00-85M14	15					Boalloy. M type reno. for dedicated traffic
Type M. 30′ Box.						
32N10-33N19	110	Cravens	1974			
33N40-34N59	120	Pacton	1974			8′ 6″ high
36N00-36N64	65	Derby	1967	3608		
36N65-37N29	65	Cowlairs	1967	3609		
37N30-46N68	939	Derby	1968	3630		
46N69-48N68	200	Derby	1968	3665		
48N69-50N68	200	York	1973			
50N69-52N18	150	Adamson	1974			
52N19-55N68	350	British Rail	1978			8′ 6″ high
55N69-58N18	250	British Rail	1979			8′ 6″ high
58N19-59N68	150	Ulcon	1979			8′ 6″ high
59N69-61N18	150	McArdle	1979			8′ 6″ high
86N00	1	Adamson	1986			Prototype 40′ 2.5m wide box for FLLU425000 Series

Number series	Total	Builder	Year	BR Lot	BR Diag	Notes
Type P. 20′ Insulated.						
20P01	1					
80P00	1	Mickleover	1966	3583		
80P01	1	Duralumin	1966	3584		
80P02	1	Cravens		3597		Not built.
80P03-80P22	20	Mickleover	1966	3612	3/280	
80P23-80P42	20	Duralumin	1967	3613	3/281	
80P43-80P82	40	Duralumin	1967	3623	3/281	
80P83-81P02	20	Duralumin	1967	3624	3/281	
81P03-81P22	20	Viking Marine	1968	3671		
81P23-81P42	20	Concargo	1968	3678		
81P43-81P92	50	Concargo	1969	3683		
81P93-82P92	100	Derby	1969	3684		
Type R. Modified Insulated.						
74R70-74R99	30	Mod. Coat-bridge	1981-4			30′ long, 8′ 6″. Ex-N type (random numbers)
82R00	1	Mickleover	1964	3492		Also designated type CAF. Orig. No. 001R
82R01	1	Mickleover	1964	3519		
Type S (I). 20′ Side door.						
70S00-70S49	50	Cravens	1967	3611	3/310	
70S50-70S74	25	Derby	1968	3674		
Type S (II). 20′ Open top.						
40S00	1					
90S00-90S99	100	Moores	1983			
Type T. 20′ Flat for Steel Coil.						
45T00	1	Forgecraft	1967	3634		
45T01	1	Tillotson	1967	3636		
46T01-47T30	130	N.W.Trailers	1973			
87T12-88T61	150	N.W.Trailers	1974			
Type V. 30′ Open skeletal (ex-N type).						
85V72-86V93	122					8′ 6″ wide
Type W. 20′ Open (modified H type with load bearing sides).						
30W09-32W09	200	Mod. BR, Glasgow	1969			8′ 6″ wide
Type X. Modified and Prototype.						
26X01-26X20	19					Hatch loading
89X00-89X19	20	McArdles	1983			Converted from N type to open top.
95X19	1		m.1979			30′ flat, ex-91C24
95X20-95X21	2		m.1979/80			30′ loading ramps, ex-54C44 & 56J20
95X29-95X30	2	N.W.Trailer	1982/3			40′ prototype Flat
95X31	1	Cravens/Tasker	1982			40′ prototype Boalloy
95X40	1	York Marine	1984			40′ prototype with side access
95X57	1					20′ Inspectors tackle, ex-13L73
96X00-96X01	2	Commercial Coach	1967	3649		
96X02	1	Derby	1967	3677		
97X00	1	Derby	1967	3648		
97X01	1	Derby	1969	3695		
98X00	1	Derby	1967	3650	3/320	
Type Y. 30′ Open (modified K type with load bearing sides).						
68Y81-69Y80	100	St Rollox	1969			8′ 6″ wide: Ex-68K81- 69K80
Type Z. Freightliner Caboose.						
99Z00-99Z01	2	Derby	1965	3565	3/490	
99Z02-99Z06	5	Derby	1966	3572	3/490	
Miscellaneous: Demonstrator tank containers.						
LLG17116B	1	Darham Ind.	1965	3570	3/740	15T/4000 gall general purpose tank
LLG17117B	1	Darham Ind.	1965	3571	3/741	15T/3600 gall general purpose tank
LP17199B	1	Interconsult	1965	3551	3/742	15T/750 cu. ft. Pressure tank

Chapter 9

Containerisation

Company Trains

From the start of the Freightliner story a number of companies were quick to see the benefits of the new system. An attempt to carry parcels traffic between London and Glasgow using the system was tried by 'Tartan Arrow' and terminals were opened at Kentish Town (London) and Dalmarnock (Glasgow). Unfortunately the service was not as successful as was first hoped and it did not survive for long. A more successful venture was tried by the Ford Motor Company and on 20th August 1968 the first 'company' container train was instigated. This followed lengthy negotiations and detailed planning between BR, BR Shipping and International services, and the Belgian and the German Railways. Running between Halewood (Liverpool) and Harwich Parkeston Quay for onward shipment to Zeebrugge the train conveyed Ford Motor Company parts destined for Genk (Belgium), Cologne and Zarlouis (Germany).

This service of production line material developed after the decision by the Ford Motor Company to produce the 'European' car in the form of their Escort and Capri models, using their various plants for specialised output of component parts.

Loadings from the outset were good and represented movement of upwards of sixty 30 ft containers a day in each direction over the Parkeston-Zeebrugge container route. This daily flow was divided into 42 containers from Halewood, and the remainder from Stratford or Dagenham. The plan allowed a transit time of 22 hours from Halewood to the Belgian plant at Genk and this schedule was maintained with ease through both summer and winter operating conditions.

In 1970 another contract was gained from the Rootes (Chrysler) Company at Coventry. A Freightliner type service was booked to operate in each direction between

Ten Ford Motor Company containers in sidings at Liverpool when brand new. They were used on the Company Freightliner train between Halewood and Harwich Parkeston Quay for conveying motor car components to the Ford factory at Genk in Belgium.
Colin J. Marsden Collection

Linwood and the Ryton and Stoke factories at Coventry. For this shuttle service some 80 Freightliner wagons were constructed to run in 16-wagon trains twice daily in each direction conveying 30 ft containers of which there were 231 units in the pool. Panels and gearboxes, which were made at Linwood, were sent to Coventry to be incorporated into new cars and in the opposite direction came transmission units from the Stoke factory to Linwood. Additional sidings space was constructed at the Scottish terminal and a 200 hp Butlers straddle carrier was installed to handle the containers. At the Coventry end an Allen Crane, spanning two rail tracks and two road lanes, was installed at Gosford Green for transfer of containers to road trailers for the final stage of their journey to the factory. Unfortunately the economics of motor car manufacture changed considerably in the 1970s and '80s and neither of these traffic flows now exist.

The 16.30 Harwich Quay-Halewood Ford Motor Company Freightliner passing Boreham, near Chelmsford with Class 47 No.47162 in charge on 22nd May 1980. These trains were known locally as 'blue trains' owing to the distinctive livery carried by the containers.
Michael J. Collins

A Harwich Parkeston Quay-Halewood train of Ford Motor Company containers passes Ardleigh, north of Colchester, on 23rd March 1982 behind Class 47 No.47115.
Michael J. Collins

Other Goods

The first ever custom-built containerised rail-road service for solid fuel started in April 1969. Five 400 ton trains were operated every fortnight between the National Coal Board's coke ovens at Derwenthaugh, near Gateshead and Wakefield in the West Riding. The train ran more regularly from Spring 1970 when Cobra Containers Ltd purchased 20 Crane Freuhauf Bulktainers for use on this 'Cobra Container' service between the North East and Wakefield.

Again, due to changing economics in the fuel industry the train was discontinued in May 1985 and the coke ovens closed shortly afterwards.

Later came the transport of bricks by rail. The London Brick Company (LBC) had a complex of works near Bedford. For several years LBC had been operating from its Calvert Works a simple partially-mechanised rail system which was devised to produce working data for the transport of bricks by rail with the aim of designing a more sophisticated system later. As a result of this experience the

Class 81 No.81018 races through Shap on 2nd April 1974 heading north with Chrysler car components destined for the Linwood plant. The photograph was taken over a month before the introduction of full electric working over the WCML to Glasgow on 6th May 1974.
Brian Morrison

Class 46 No.46038 shunts the Cobra coke depot at Wakefield on 26th February 1982.
Chris Davies'

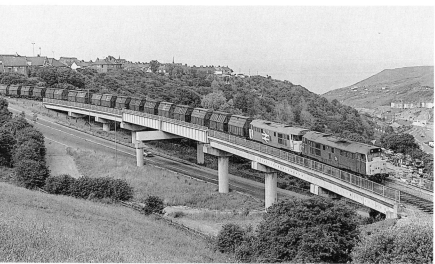

Class 45 No.45042 passes Burton Salmon with the 13.45 Wakefield-Derwenthaugh Cobra coke empties on 11th August 1981. The containers are mounted on privately owned FEV wagons.
Paul D. Shannon

A train load of the distinctive shaped containers used for the transit of potash in the North East. Class 31s Nos 31278 and 31183 pass Skinningrove with a Middlesbrough Goods-Boulby working on 15th July 1986.
Paul D. Shannon

company worked to evolve the Fletliner container and constructed the rail-container terminal at its Stewartby Works. Technical advice was afforded by Freightliners but the project was funded entirely with LBC capital. The partnership was marked by the adoption of the 'Fletliner' brand name (LBC was the sole manufacturer of Fletton bricks). The terminal at Stewartby was 1,220 ft long and was made up of two rail tracks, a roadway and a stacking area with a 20-ton crane spanning the whole complex. In essence it resembled a miniature Freightliner terminal and was, in fact, the first such terminal to be owned and operated privately.

Fletliner Operations

Each container was loaded within the works complex with between 6,750 and 7,250 bricks. Containers were then loaded by the gantry crane onto Freightliner wagons which operated as block trains on a twenty-four hour cycle. A train normally consisted of 15 wagons – each one loaded with three 20 ft containers of bricks. Thus, 45 containers constituted a single train load hauling a total of approximately 315,000 bricks. This was enough for about eight average houses. At first one train left Stewartby five days a week, one section of it bound for the Freightliner terminal at Manchester (Trafford Park) where a portion was detached and sent onwards to Liverpool (Garston). The route outward was via Bedford, Wellingborough, Wigston Junction and Nuneaton. The empties returned via the WCML and Bletchley.

As shown in *Table 7*, following pilot operation between Stewartby and Manchester and Liverpool the LBC introduced a short-haul service in Spring 1974 between Stewartby and King's Cross goods. The Fletliner concept provided a highly mechanised distribution system which allowed LBC to deliver large quantities of bricks under the slogan "Works to Wall". It allowed 3.2 million bricks a week to be despatched to the three centres.

Table 7 LBC Fletliner Train Schedule Summer 1974

Stewartby-LBC-Terminal	Dep. 14.28
Manchester Trafford Park F.L. Terminal	Arr. 19.53
	Dep. 23.20
Liverpool-Garston-F.L. Terminal	Arr. 00.38
Stewartby-LBC-Terminal	Arr. 06.50
Stewartby-LBC-Terminal	Dep. 21.58
King's Cross FL Terminal	Arr. 23.52
	Dep. 09.58
Stewartby-LBC-Terminal	Arr. 11.46

Mixed Trains

Freightliner had a brief flirtation with the idea of operating a Freightliner section at the rear of a passenger train in 1969/70. A Freightliner section conveying Irish traffic ran from Cardiff to Fishguard three days a week at the rear of the 08.00 boat train from Paddington. On 26th March 1984 the idea was tried again when the 13.55 Aberdeen-Inverness and 17.40 Inverness-Wick passenger trains were made into a mixed passenger and Freightliner train. The freight vehicles carried containers for Sutherland Transport

Ltd. Four Freightliner vehicles were involved – allocated to pool No.1081 based at Aberdeen . They were FJB type 60 ft wagons – very similar to conventional Freightliner wagons but were equipped with normal buffing arrangements at each end. They were fitted with a vacuum through pipe so that they could operate with vacuum braked passenger stock. Again, this mixed service ran for some months but faded into oblivion during 1985.

The Litterliners

After many years of succesful running, the brick trains referred to above ceased running because of changes in the economics of the construction industry and loss to road transport. A scheme was put forward to use the redundant terminal at Stewartby and at the same time reclaim vast acres of land made waste by extraction of clay. This was to be done by by filling the pits with household refuse. The scheme was devised by the London Midland Region of BR in partnership with London Brick Land Developments Ltd (LBLDL) and the Greater London Council (GLC). It involved construction of a railhead at Brent adjacent to the one-time diesel locomotive running shed at Cricklewood on the Midland Main Line. Here, household refuse from several London boroughs is compacted and loaded into containers. From Brent train loads of containers (dubbed 'Litterliners') are run on Freightliner flats to worked-out clay pits owned by the LBC at Stewartby. The refuse is used as infill material being disposed of in scientifically controlled conditions. The land made available by filling in the pits will eventually be restored to productive use as either farmland or for recreational purposes. Another similar scheme was set up by the GLC which runs household refuse in containers from Brentford to Appleford, near Didcot, and yet another runs trains from a depot at Hillingdon up the Great Central line to Calvert. In 1982 the facilities at Calvert were considered by Avon County Council who then made a decision to pursue an 'out-of-county' waste disposal scheme. It took another two years to process the necessary planning procedures before one set of wagons purchased from Powell Duffryn was used to service the waste transfer stations at Bath, Bristol and Westerleigh. From here the household waste is transported the 150 km to the Shanks & McEwan disposal site at Calvert.

Class 25s Nos 25266 and 25315 recorded between Bedford St Johns and Bedford Midland stations with the 13.21 Stewartby-Garston Fletliner of 28th July 1981. Unfortunately, this traffic has now been lost to road haulage.

Paul D. Shannon

Class 47 No.47206 passes Persley, Aberdeen, on 14th May 1984 with the 13.45 Aberdeen-Inverness passenger train. Behind the locomotive is a single Freightliner wagon carrying a pair of containers for onward transit to Wick and Thurso.

Cyril J. Lofthus

The Hendon-Stewartby "Easidispose" household refuse train passes Bedford St Johns behind Class 31s Nos 31226 and 31198 on 27th July 1988. BR see the "Litterliners" as an area of considerable potential growth in traffic, especially in the crowded South East of England where land suitable for tipping is at a premium.

Michael J. Collins

In Raillfreight Construction livery Class 47 No.47079 (formerly *G. J. Churchward*) passes Foxhall Junction, Didcot, with the Calvert-Avon "Litterliner" empties on 7th April 1988.

Michael J. Collins

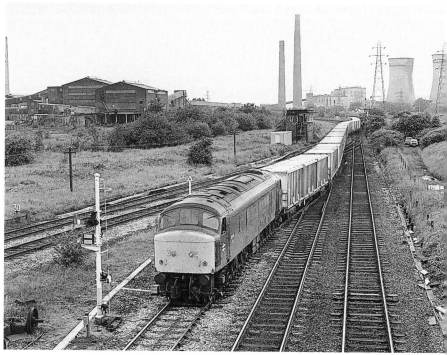

In Manchester, too, household refuse is disposed of by rail. The Greater Manchester schemes, however, do not rely on the idea of compacting raw refuse direct into containers as they do in London. They have opted to pulverise the material and gravity load it through the top of the containers. The first Greater Manchester scheme to come into operation was from Dean Lane, in the northern suburbs of Manchester to the Wimpey owned waste site at Appley Bridge near Wigan. In October 1985 a joint service has been run serving the Brindle Heath, Salford, waste plant. The combined service operates seven days a week conveying weekly some 4,200 tonnes of household rubbish for disposal. The other service in the Manchester area was runs from Northenden in South Manchester, again to Appley Bridge. This service was inaugurated in Summer 1982 and it can be deduced that today up to three trains a day are scheduled to be unloaded at Appley Bridge. The basic pattern is that a train can be discharged and reloaded with empty containers within about two hours. This system leaves little margin for error and delay, but Railfreight believes that tight scheduling such as this example is a practical basis for future schemes.

In June 1989 a new scheme was announced for removal of waste by rail in containers. This was a partnership between Railfreight, Edinburgh District Council and Tarmac Econowaste. Trains began running five days a week from the following November between the city's Powderhall refuse disposal works and Econowaste's Kaimes landfill site situated at Kirknewton on the Edinburgh-Carstairs route.

All existing domestic waste traffic is characterised by a co-operative venture between Railfreight, local authorities and a waste disposal company. With increased pressure on available places for tipping rubbish Railfreight sees this as a growth market and is considering other schemes jointly with these companies. Road congestion, particularly in the South East, is giving rail a competitive stance, even on the short haul flows from London to Bedfordshire. It is this edge which may well see some existing road borne traffic won back by rail in addition to any brand new schemes which can be attracted.

Petfoods, Cawoods Coal and Dolofines

It was in Spring 1986 that another regular company train using the container concept was started. The flow was based on an order of privately owned PFA type bogie flats constructed by the Standard Railway Wagon Company at their works situated at Heywood, Lancashire. A second batch was completed early in 1986 and had to be stored at Heywood for some weeks. Interestingly, although they were a private build, the spare wagons were leased to Freightliner for some weeks and operated in normal services – often on the Tilbury-Glasgow service. The new train originated from the Pedigree Petfoods factory situated adjacent to the lineside at Melton Mowbray conveying pet food to a distribution and warehousing complex set up at

Welwyn Garden City. A second flow was established later in 1986 to run to the North West. At first, Heywood in Lancashire was to be the destination for the traffic but problems developed and a more suitable site was found at Ardwick, Manchester. The new service to this terminal started on 6th October 1986. Once the train has arrived at Ardwick the curtain sided containers – carried two per container flat (TOPS code PFA) , are lifted off the train by forklift truck for onward distribution by road.

During early 1986 the road haulier John G. Russell (Transport) Ltd of Gartcosh was awarded a contract from British Steel to transport 100,000 tonnes of dolofines to its Ravenscraig plant. The firm then sub-contracted British Rail to provide the trunk haul from Thrislington Quarry, near Ferryhill County Durham, to Russell's rail-connected depot at Gartcosh. The firm had invested £1 million matched by a Section 8 grant from the Scottish Office to equip its depot with container handling. Dolofines – a flux used in the steel making process – were loaded directly into Russell's containers at the quarry – and was made up into a train load carrying 400 tonnes in 19 open demountable containers. Every weekday a complete train left Ferryhill for Gartcosh. From there all containers would be delivered to Ravenscraig within two hours of arrival in Scotland. The empty containers were returned to Ferryhill for refilling by an overnight service. More recently Gartcosh has become the receiving point for a coal flow from Healey Mills transported by rail in open containers on 4-wheel flat wagons.

During December 1986 delivery commenced of an order of 108 two-axle container carrying wagons, again built by Standard Railway Wagon. Once again it was a private venture which harnessed the container principal for the bulk haul. The new wagons were to be operated by Cawoods between South Wales and Ellesmere Port for coal traffic. They are similar in design to the BR owned FPA wagons except that they have raised ends. Again the concept was successful and the black wagons carrying yellow containers full of coal have become a feature of the Welsh Marches line heading northwards from Newport. Later, similar wagons were used in Scotland. They enabled Aberdeen to rejoin the container network when the town's coal depot was moved from the outer city site at Kittybrewster to a central site next to existing freight facilities and the dock complex. It was expected to save 1,500 lorry movements a year. The new site was operated by John Russell Ltd, the then new Railfreight agent in Aberdeen for coal products. It was a little ironic that they bought one of the Freightliner cranes from the closed depot which they had used in the movement of bulk coal containers from the sidings to the adjacent coal depot. The coal, mostly from Kellingly and Markham Main collieries moves overnight on Speedlink Distribution trains but the new facilities are certainly reported to be in the market for container traffic in general.

On 20th January 1988 the first of a national chain of coal-concentration depots was re-opened at British Coal's West Drayton Depot. Originally opened in 1963, the depot had been substantially modernised and equipped to receive coal from South Wales in containers belonging to John G. Russell. They found that the use of containers enhanced product quality, received as if collected direct from the colliery screens.

In Summer 1988 a new partnership was forged between Freightliner and McPhersons Transport (Aberdour) Ltd to open up markets in the North of Scotland. The operation was based on Elgin station where an existing rail-mounted crane was installed to offload containers from road vehicles to rail wagons and vice versa. Loaded rail container wagons were then incorporated into freight services to be taken down to Coatbridge to connect with services to and from Southern England, the Midlands and Europe via Felixstowe.

Bimodal Systems

It has been the intention so far in this chapter to highlight developments which have taken place over the years to harness the container concept by both private industry and BR. It is a fact though that Railfreight Distribution have not been standing still in recent years. Over the last few years distribution by Railfreight has enjoyed a sustained and dramatic growth record. In 1986, for example, business with food and drink manufacturers alone increased by over 30%. This growth has been achieved through producing some imaginative solutions to distribution problems in particular by creating contracts which are tailored to suit each individual customer's needs. After several years of research, development and testing Railfreight have commercially implemented a number of bimodal sytems to meet these individual customer needs. One of the catalysts for this thinking was the projected amalgamation of the Speedlink Distribution and Freightliner enterprises. This finally took place in Autumn 1988. One of the problems of railfreight is that nearly everything which is conveyed by rail – except perhaps some bulk shipments such as oil, coal and minerals – has to be loaded onto a lorry at some stage in its journey. That takes time and money and many manufacturing firms consider it as just another link in a chain that can go wrong. It would be far easier, they argue, to keep the merchandise in the lorry to save hassle.

It has long been argued that a distribution service capable of combining the best features of rail and road haulage would be a winner. Nothing can match rail transport over longer distances for speed, efficiency and environmental gains. Traffic moves mainly at night, safely and securely, at speeds up to 75mph. In addition, each load that can be attracted to rail means fewer lorries to pollute our environment and cause congestion on the roads. On the other hand, using local road distribution for transit to and from terminals coupled with overnight transit by rail for the long haul, offers a system boasting economy, flexibility and reliability with the added advantage of door-to-door delivery.

At an exhibition staged at Willesden in October 1987 three new systems harnessing the container approach were unveiled. Each was designed to circumvent the problems mentioned above and were marketed as bimodal systems.

'MiniLink' is a small demountable body system which utilizes a four wheel chassis to transfer entire vehicle bodies from road to rail in just one minute without the need for heavy cranage. Originally developed in Sweden, but adapted to suit the constraints of the British market, it is utilised as a van, flatbed or liquid tanker. There is 520 cubic feet of usable space with securing points to keep the load safe and steady.The complete merchandise-bearing section is lifted from the lorry onto a rail wagon without any interference to the contents. As the name implies 'MaxiLink' is a larger version of the 'MiniLink' idea but the transfer vehicle employs an air bag lift and side sliding mechanism to transfer the cargo carrying sections from road to rail in just six minutes. The 'Trailer Train' was shown at the same exhibition and is a very ingenious device. This places an articulated trailer on a set of rail wheels. It has been tested on

In the correct Railfreight Distribution livery Class 47 No.47317 passes Washstons Crossing with a westbound containerised petfood service from Melton Mowbray on 13th April 1988.

John C. Baker

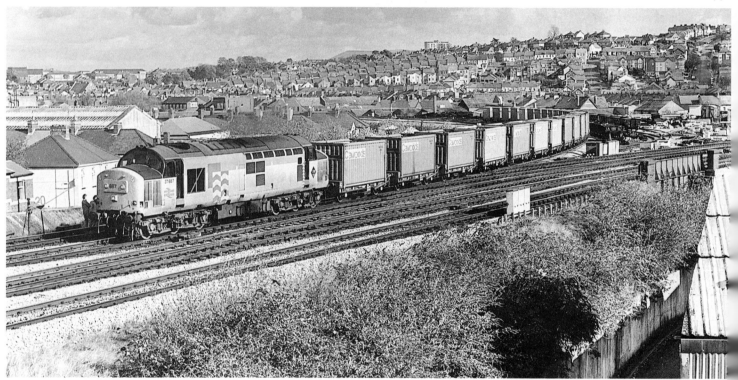

Refurbished Class 37 No.37887 (of the Railfreight Petroleum sub-sector) passes Maindee West Junction, Newport, with the 08.00 Ellesmere Port-Abercwmboi "Cawoods" coal empties on 27th October 1988. The distinctive yellow livery applied to these containers has considerably brightened the railway scene in these parts.

Michael J. Collins

One of the FPA coal container conversions carried out at BREL Doncaster photographed on 7th December 1984.

Colin J. Marsden

both road and rail at speeds considerably higher than its normal service speed, and has proved to be entirely safe and stable in both modes of operation. The trailer train has made several successful experimental runs from Cambridgeshire conveying pet food products. Transfer to rail can be at any point where rail access is available and where there is a suitable concrete pad for the road tractor to manoeuvre the trailer. No special equipment is required for the transfer as all energy is provided from the tractor's pneumatic system.

Swap-Bodies

As this book was being finalised Railfreight Distribution announced their intentions to launch BR's first 90 mph freight train. The idea was to use swap-bodies – demountable containers similar to ISO containers but more economically constructed. They are commonly used on the Continent including railway inter modal traffic. They have not yet been used much in the UK but when the single market arrives in 1992 and the Channel Tunnel comes into use shortly afterwards they will undoubtably proliferate. Railfreight's new service, linking Harwich, the North West and Glasgow will be run exclusively for swap-bodies. With a Class 90 providing traction, the 20-wagon train will leave Harwich at approximately 09.00 and travel via the North London Line to arrive at Warrington at about 13.30. There, about half the train (carrying the North West traffic) will be detached. The train will then restart and is booked to arrive in Glasgow at just after 17.00. Average speed for the entire journey including the pause at Warrington is set to be about 57 mph. Return from Glasgow will be around 20.00 and,

after a pause again at Warrington, arrival back at Harwich will be at about 05.00.

To market the new swap-body trains BR have entered into a collaborative relationship with the experienced Continental firms of Intercontainer and Kombi-Novatrans. The only economical rail wagon that can accommodate the popular C22 size of European swap-body within the British loading gauge is French Railways (SNCF) Mulifret, which was designed with the constraints of the BR loading gauge in mind for post tunnel through running. These wagons are passed by SNCF to run at 87.5 mph and BR considers that they can easily run at 90mph over here.

This exciting development underlines the importance of bi-modal transport systems in the competitive transport market of today. Railfreight Distribution see the swap-body concept combined with their Minilink and Maxilink systems as the way forward into the year 2000. This is why they are anxious to get experience of swap-body technology before the advent of the Channel Tunnel. It looks as if the container principal, based on a derivative of the ISO container, will be the major inter-modal transport tool of the 21st century. What vision it took to recognise that fact twenty-five years ago when the Freightliner trains first took to the rails.

Not often publicised, seen or photographed is the bullion container train which carries highly valuable cargoes for the Royal Mint to different parts of the system. The train is recorded leaving Doncaster heading for King's Cross goods on 21st August 1981 behind Class 31 No.31185. Note the brake van at the rear used for carrying armed security guards with the train.

Colin J. Marsden

One of the MiniLink containers demonstrated on a Speedlink Distribution Leyland lorry at a special exhibition held at Ripple Lane in October 1987.

Michael J. Collins

One of the MaxiLink road/rail containers demonstrated on a Railfreight Distribution Volvo lorry at Ripple Lane during October 1987.

Michael J. Collins

Class 08 No.08834 shunts MaxiLink containers on a PFA rail wagon at Ripple Lane on 15th October 1987.

Colin J. Marsden

60
111

Solent Services

The 07.10 Coatbridge-Southampton Marine passes Kennington, Oxford, on 1st October 1988 behind Class 47 No.47378. The bridge in the right background took the one-time GWR branch to Thame over the River Thames.

Michael J. Collins

Framed in the famous bracket signal which guards Aynho Junction is the 07.10 Coatbridge-Southampton Maritime service. Traction was being supplied on this occasion, 17th September 1988, by Class 47 No.47350 *British Petroleum*.

Michael J. Collins

The 15.06 SO service from Ripple Lane to Southampton Maritime accelerates away from its point of origin on 10th September 1988 behind Class 47 No.47333. Above the locomotive can be seen the offices of Ripple Lane traction servicing depot and the Freightliner terminal can be seen on the horizon above the oil tanks. Note the OCL container on the wagon immediately behind the locomotive.

Michael J. Collins

A Southampton-Leeds extra Freightliner suffers a signal check at Basingstoke station on 27th March 1982. Traction for the service was supplied by Class 47 No.47197 on this occasion.

Michael J. Collins

This Holyhead to Southampton Freightliner behind Class 33 No.33107 is approaching the Solent port from a strange direction. Diverted because of engineering works the train has travelled from Basingstoke via Andover, Laverstock North Junction and Romsey. It is rejoining the main Bournemouth line at Redbridge and will arrive at Millbrook Terminal in just a few minutes.

Michael J. Collins

A Coatbridge-Southampton Maritime Freightliner passes Bescot, near Birmingham, behind Class 86 No.86412 on 4th October 1986. The train will change to diesel traction in Bescot Yard.

John Whitehouse

Approaching Banbury is a well loaded Freightliner bound for Southampton with Class 56 No.56062 in charge. Traction will be changed at either Banbury or Oxford.

Dr L. A. Nixon

East Coast Traffic

Recently transferred to Stratford from Inverness, Class 47 No.47430 still wears its 'ScotRail' colours as it roars past Marks Tey Yard with a Stratford-Felixstowe Freightliner on 22nd October 1988. Most of the payload consists of steel coil in Seawheel containers.

Michael J. Collins

A pristine celebrity locomotive hauling a Freightliner service. Class 47 No.47522 *Doncaster Enterprise*, in LNER apple green livery, passes Colchester on 30th August 1988 with a special Freightliner for Felixstowe. Stabled on the left is Class 03 No. 03059 (D2059) (also in green livery) which is now preserved in the Isle of Wight.

Michael J. Collins

Seen on the single track Felixstowe branch, just south of Westerfield Junction is Class 47 No.47007 *Stratford* hauling the 20.07 Coatbridge-Felixstowe North service on 26th March 1988. The two overnight trains between Scotland and Felixstowe usually load well and this occasion was no exception.

Michael J. Collins

This piece of railway is the nearest to the author's home and he can lay in bed at night and hear the Freightliner trains rumble over this viaduct! Class 37s Nos 37107 and 37084 take a Felixstowe-Garston service over Seven Arches Viaduct, Stanway near Colchester, on 16th February 1988.

Michael J. Collins

A bird's eye view from the top of the grain silos at Haughley Junction. The 20.54 Coatbridge-Felixstowe joins the GE main line for the run down to Ipswich where it has to reverse to gain the Felixstowe branch. In charge, on 31st August 1989, is the unusual combination of Class 31 No.31106 working in multiple with Class 37 No.37154. There had obviously been a failure en route because this train is normally booked for a pair of Class 37s.
Michael J. Collins

Having passed from Essex into Suffolk by crossing the River Stour at Manningtree Class 47 No.47096 hammers up the grade to Brantham with a Willesden-Felixstowe service. The Essex town of Manningtree can be seen in the valley behind the train.
Michael J. Collins

A pre-electrification view of Mistley, on the Harwich branch, as Class 47 No.47150 *Henry Ford* passes by with a trip Freightliner working from Ipswich Yard to Harwich Parkeston Quay. The signal box on the right is now preserved at the East Anglian Railway Museum situated at Chappel and Wakes Colne station in Essex.
Michael J. Collins

The modern scene in East Anglia. Class 86/4s Nos 86416 *Wigan Pier* and 86412 *Elizabeth Garratt Anderson* pass Hatfield Peverel with a Garston-Felixstowe working on 19th July 1989.
Michael J. Collins

Irish Stew

Another load of containers bound for Ireland as a Willesden-Holyhead Freightliner rounds the Northampton Loop approaching Hunsbury Hill Tunnel on 25th July 1984 with an unidentified Class 86 in charge.

Dr L. A. Nixon

Alongside Conway Castle Class 47 No.47381 races past with a Freightliner for Holyhead on 8th August 1983. Note the train spotting seagull on top of the signal!

Dr L. A. Nixon

Following the demise of the Class 40s members of Class 45 started to perform on the North Wales main line on Freightliner duties. Class 45 No.45060 *Sherwood Forester* (now preserved) races through Rhyl station with the 14.40 Lawley Street-Holyhead Freightliner service on 17th August 1984.

Larry Goddard

On 22nd February 1985, a member of the Royal Family visited Chester, and everything was shut down until the Royal Train had departed as empty stock. This was followed by a procession of trains – all running late by this time. This included Class 47 No.47366 which ran through the station at 12.45 with the re-timed Holyhead-Willesden Freightliner no doubt conveying much Guinness for consumption in England. This locomotive was named *The Institute of Civil Engineers* at Liverpool Lime Street on 22nd May 1986 and it also held the distinction of being the last Class 47 to retain the two tone green livery once associated with the class.

Larry Goddard

Class 40 No.40158 speeds down the North Wales main line from Llandulas on 4th June 1983. The long downhill run from Llysfaen often provided the Class 40s with the opportunity of accelerating container trains up to their maximum permitted speed of 75 mph.

Larry Goddard

Class 40 No.40050 passes Frodsham station on 25th March 1983 with the 15.45 Trafford Park-Holyhead Freightliner service. The Class 40s held a long association with powering Freightliner trains along this section of line.

Geoff Dowling